The Mysterious & Unknown

The Curse
of King Tut

by William W. Lace

ReferencePoint
Press™

San Diego, CA

For more information, contact
ReferencePoint Press, Inc.
PO Box 27779
San Diego, CA 92198
www.ReferencePointPress.com

Picture credits:
AP/Wide World Photos: 7, 9, 22, 36, 44, 59, 63, 67, 69, 75, 81, 91
The British Museum: 11, 41
Department of Egyptian Antiquities: 13
Landov: 5, 12, 25, 57, 70, 77, 86, 93
Steve Zmina: 46–47
Wikipedia: 31, 33
Yorck Project: 14

Series design and book layout:
Amy Stirnkorb

LIBRARY OF CONGRESS CATALOGING-IN-PUBLICATION DATA

Lace, William W.
 The curse of King Tut / by William W. Lace.
   p. cm. -- (Mysterious & unknown)
 Includes bibliographical references and index.
 ISBN-13: 978-1-60152-024-1 (hardback)
 ISBN-10: 1-60152-024-7 (hardback)
 1. Tutankhamen, King of Egypt--Tomb--Juvenile literature. 2. Blessing and cursing--Egypt--Juvenile literature. I. Title.
DT87.5.L33 2007
932'.014--dc22
                                                                              2007010987

CONTENTS

FOREWORD

"Strange is our situation here upon earth."
—*Albert Einstein*

Since the beginning of recorded history, people have been perplexed, fascinated, and even terrified by events that defy explanation. While science has demystified many of these events, such as volcanic eruptions and lunar eclipses, some continue to remain outside the scope of the provable. Do UFOs exist? Are people abducted by aliens? Can some people see into the future? These questions and many more continue to puzzle, intrigue, and confound despite the enormous advances of modern science and technology.

It is these questions, phenomena, and oddities that Reference-Point Press's *The Mysterious & Unknown* series is committed to exploring. Each volume examines historical and anecdotal evidence as well as the most recent theories surrounding the topic in debate. Fascinating primary source quotes from scientists, experts, and eyewitnesses, as well as in-depth sidebars further inform the text. Full-color illustrations and photos add to each book's visual appeal. Finally, source notes, a bibliography, and a thorough index provide further reference and research support. Whether for research or the curious reader, *The Mysterious & Unknown* series is certain to satisfy those fascinated by the unexplained.

INTRODUCTION

The Wings of Death

On the afternoon of November 26, 1922, archaeologist Howard Carter stood before a sealed doorway at the end of an underground stone tunnel in Egypt's Valley of the Kings. Watching closely was his patron, the British nobleman Lord Carnarvon. Carnarvon's daughter, Lady Evelyn Herbert, was also there as was Carter's colleague A.R. "Pecky" Callender.

They were poised to learn whether or not, beyond the door, lay what Carter had been seeking for years—the tomb of Tutankhamen—"King Tut," pharaoh of Egypt more than 3,000 years earlier. Hopes were high, but hopes had been dashed frequently over the 15 years that Carnarvon had financed Carter's search. Most experts, after all, said there were no more important discoveries to be made in the Valley of the Kings.

Carter used an iron bar to make a small hole in the door's upper left-hand corner, then enlarged it to the point where he could insert a candle and peer through. At first he was speechless with amazement, and when the others asked him if he could see

Archaeologist Howard Carter discovered the tomb of King Tut in the Valley of the Kings in November of 1922.

anything, it was all he could do to say, "Yes, wonderful things."[1] He had discovered something that many said no longer existed—a virtually intact tomb of an Egyptian pharaoh.

Careful Work

Over the next three months, Carter and his team carefully cataloged the hundreds of items contained in the first two rooms—the antechamber and annex. Every statue, jar, bead, and scrap of leather was numbered, photographed, and a record kept of where they had been found.

Finally, on February 17, 1923, the time came for another momentous opening. As more than 20 people—the cream of Egyptian and British society—looked on, Carter began chipping away at the door behind which he thought was Tutankhamen's final resting place. As before, he made a hole large enough to shine a light through. Before him, he later wrote, was "a solid wall of gold. . . . It was, beyond any question, the sepulchral [burial] chamber in which we stood, for here, towering above us was one of the great gilt shrines in which kings were laid."[2]

Less than two months after Tutankhamen's burial chamber had been entered, disaster struck. Carnarvon, whose fortune and whose faith in Carter had made the tomb's discovery possible, was dead. With his death was born the story that the tomb was cursed and that those associated with violating the pharaoh's slumber would share Carnarvon's fate.

The Curse Story

Newspapers began to spread the story of the curse. Reports claimed that a stone tablet had been found in the tomb bearing the inscription "Death will slay with his wings whoever disturbs

the peace of the pharaoh."[3] Another report mentioned a curse carved above the tomb's door: "Let the hand raised against my form be withered! Let them be destroyed who attack my name, my foundation, my effigies, the images like unto me."[4]

Yet nowhere in Carter's meticulous records is there any mention of either the stone tablet or of the curse carved above the door. No member of the team reported having seen them. None of the thousands of photographs of the tomb's artifacts show them.

Carter denied they ever existed. He denied the possibility of a curse. Yet, over the years, more and more people associated with the tomb died under mysterious circumstances. With each death, the legend grew. Critics have tried to explain the deaths as coincidences. Scientists have come up with several possible natural explanations. No explanation, however, has been able to entirely dispel the notion that a curse set down so many centuries ago had extended its hand to strike down those who disturbed the king's rest.

Egyptian tombs were sometimes rumored to have curses. This tomb, belonging to dentists who served royalty, had a curse inscription warning that those who enter would be eaten by crocodiles and snakes.

CHAPTER 1

Prince, King, Mummy

Tutankhamen ruled Egypt as pharaoh for 10 largely undistinguished years. He was neither a warrior nor a statesman. And yet, because of his tomb—and the curse supposedly laid on it—he is the best-known person in more than 5,000 years of Egyptian civilization.

Despite his fame, however, very little is known about Tutankhamen. Egyptologists are unsure as to when he was born and even who his parents were. His birth most likely took place in the tenth year of the reign of Akhenaton, sometime about 1341 B.C., but whether or not he was Akhenaton's son is a matter of debate.

Some experts claim he was Akhenaton's half brother, son of Amenhotep III and Tiye, his Great Royal Wife (there being no ancient Egyptian word for queen) in their older years. Others claim that he was not of royal birth but based his claim to the throne through marriage to one of the daughters of Akhenaton and his

This limestone relief depicts Akhenaton and his family worshipping Aten, the sun god. Some experts claim Tutankhamen was Akhenaton's brother yet others believe he was his son. Tutankhamen's claim to the throne remains a mystery.

Great Royal Wife Nefertiti. The prevailing theory, however, is that he was indeed Akhenaton's son by Kiya, a secondary wife.

Whether or not he was Tutankhamen's father, Akhenaton had a profound influence on the future king and on Egyptian history. He was born Amenhotep, second son of Amenhotep III, and became heir to the throne on the death of his older brother.

A New Religion

At this point in Egyptian history, the most supreme of their many gods was Amun, once only a local god of the capital city of Thebes, the present-day Luxor, but who had been linked to the ancient sun god Ra. The priests of Amun-Ra had amassed such wealth that their power began to rival that of the pharaohs. Perhaps it was for this reason that Amenhotep III began to shift his allegiance to another god, Aten, who was a manifestation of Ra symbolized by the sun.

When Amenhotep III's son became pharaoh, he carried the worship of Aten to extremes, changing his name to Akhenaton, or "He Who Is Beneficial to Aten." He proclaimed Aten as the only god and set about to eliminate all others. He encountered such fierce resistance from the people, stirred up by the priests of Amun-Ra, that he left Thebes to build a new capital, Akhetaton, on the Nile River to the north.

It was in Akhetaton that Tutankhamen, whose original name was Tutankhaten, was born. His mother died shortly afterward, and he seems to have been brought up under the protection of his grandmother, Tiye, and her brother Ay, father of Nefertiti. It is even possible that his life was in danger from Nefertiti, who intended for herself or one of her six daughters to inherit the throne.

Akhenaton died after 17 years on the throne. The last years of his life and the period immediately afterward are difficult to document. Another pharaoh, Smenkhkare, evidently ruled prior to Tutankhamen, but it is far from clear who he was. He may have been Tutankhamen's older brother, and some have speculated that Smenkhkare was actually Nefertiti, who had given herself a man's name and ruled alongside her husband.

The Boy King

At any rate, Smenkhkare and Nefertiti soon disappeared from history, their fates unknown, and the seven-year-old Tutankhamen became pharaoh. About the same time as his coronation, he was married to his slightly older half sister Ankhesenpaaten, third daughter of Akhenaton and Nefertiti. He was ruler in name only, the affairs of the kingdom being directed by his great-uncle Ay and the army general Horemheb, both of whom were eventually to become pharaoh. It was probably these two men who, early in the reign, decided to bring unity to Egypt by moving the capital back to Thebes and restoring Amun to supremacy. Accordingly, the royal couple abandoned Akhetaton, and the young ruler changed his name to Tutankhamen.

The remainder of the reign was mostly uneventful. The temples of the old gods were restored, and Horemheb revived the country's military might, which had been allowed to deteriorate under the peace-loving Akhenaton. Carvings on a pillar erected during his reign reflect the extent to which the Egyptians welcomed a return to the old way of doing things:

Ra was the sun god who was replaced by Aten when Tut's father decided to worship only one god.

This coffin, on display at the "King Tut and the Golden Age of the Pharaohs" exhibit, belongs to King Tut's grandmother Tiye.

Now when his majesty [Tutankhamen] was crowned King the temples and the estates of the gods and goddesses from Elephantine to as far as the swamps of Lower Egypt had fallen into ruin. Their shrines had fallen down, turned into piles of rubble and overgrown with weeds. . . . The world was in chaos and all the gods had turned their backs on this land. . . . Now the gods and goddesses of this land are rejoicing in their hearts, the Lords of the temples are in joy, the provinces all rejoice and celebrate throughout this whole land because good has come back into existence.[5]

Death of Tutankhamen

Then, in a manner still not fully explained, Tutankhamen died. Until very recently it was believed that he had been murdered, killed by a blow to the back of the head. The wound had been revealed when his mummy was x-rayed in 1968. Suspicion centered on Ay, his successor, as the most likely culprit. Then in 2005 the mummy was subjected to a computerized tomography (CT) scan, which showed that the bones at the site of the wound had been broken after the body was buried, probably by the archaeologists who discovered it. Whatever the cause, the young pharaoh was dead at an age later estimated at somewhere between 16 and 19. Now it was time to prepare for the royal burial.

The ancient Egyptians held an exceptionally strong belief in life after death. Indeed, they regarded earthly life as a temporary state during which a person's actions determined whether he or she could move on to eternal life. The strength of this belief is reflected in the extraordinary care and expense taken to prepare bodies and tombs.

Belief in the afterlife was at the core of Egyptian religion and was rooted in the story of the god Osiris and his wife Isis. Osiris

In this part of the Book of the Dead, a past king meets Osiris, the Egyptian god of the dead and king of the underworld. Belief in the afterlife was at the core of Egyptian religion.

Isis is the wife of Osiris, the king of the underworld.

ruled Egypt until he was murdered by his brother Seth, who hacked his body into 14 pieces. Isis recovered all the pieces but one and breathed life into Osiris, whereupon he became king of the underworld. Meanwhile, Horus, the son of Osiris and Isis, replaced his father as ruler of the land of the living.

Journey to the Underworld

Egyptians believed that when they died, they would go to the underworld where they would be judged by Osiris. If found worthy they would enter the Fields of Hotep, an idealized mirror image of Egypt in which they would enjoy eternal life. Preservation of the earthly body, however, was necessary to maintain the heavenly existence. It was an essential link between this world and the next, and thus everything possible was done to preserve the body and to ensure it was secure—even to placing a curse on anyone who disturbed it.

The preservation and burial of a pharaoh's body was doubly important because he was considered a god—an earthly embodiment of Horus who, after death, would become Osiris. Therefore, no matter how brief or inconsequential Tutankhamen's reign was, his body would be prepared in such a way as to prepare it to be ruler of the underworld.

Preservation of the body involved mummification, a process that at the time of Tutankhamen's death had already been practiced in Egypt for more than 1,700 years. Mummification was not reserved for kings or even for the wealthy and noble. Indeed, almost everyone except criminals and slaves received some sort of preservative treatment. Otherwise, the Egyptians believed, the person's spirit would cease to exist along with the body, and this was considered the worst of fates.

Making a Mummy

Tutankhamen's body would have been taken to the embalmers' workshop, where it underwent the long process of mummification. First the embalmers used a long metal tool to extract the brain through the nostrils. The inside of the cranium was then washed out with special lotions to dissolve whatever tissue remained, after which it was filled with melted resin that eventually solidified. The brain was thrown away, the Egyptians having no concept of its function or significance.

Next, through an incision in the abdomen, the internal organs were removed. The liver, stomach, intestines, and lungs were

Companions for Eternity

People were not the only beings mummified in ancient Egypt. Mummies of pets, usually dogs or cats, have often been found in tombs with their owners. Wall carvings in these tombs show the deceased person and pet, with the name of the pet inscribed so as to assure it of eternal life along with its master or mistress. Sometimes pets were buried near their owners in small tombs of their own, complete with funerary equipment such as food and toys they might need in the next world.

The practice of burying pets may not be as cruel as it appears. Analysis of some of the mummies indicates that they were not killed at the same time as their owners died, but instead they were allowed to live out their lives before rejoining their masters.

treated with spices and carefully preserved in jars, each decorated with a figure of the appropriate goddess. Only the heart, considered by the Egyptians to be the source of a person's spirit, would eventually be returned to the body.

Once emptied, the body cavity was washed out with water and then with palm wine before being packed with the substances that would purify the body and extract all moisture. The primary ingredient was natron, a combination of salts that occurred naturally in Egypt and that had proved the most effective means of drying the body and dissolving all fatty tissue. In more elaborate burials linen bags of natron were stuffed into the body along with myrrh and frankincense to sweeten the smell. The body was then immersed in natron for 70 days, the salt being changed periodically when it became damp.

After the drying period, the natron and other materials were removed. The inside of the body cavity was coated with resin as a preservative, and the heart—now dried and wrapped in linen—was restored. The embalmers then stuffed the cavity with resin-soaked linen to maintain its shape before closing the incision.

The Wrapping

At this point, the body of Tutankhamen was ready to be wrapped. The process involved hundreds of yards of the finest linen bandages. Each finger and toe was wrapped separately, then placed into golden sheaths. The arms were wrapped, adorned with golden bracelets, and folded over the chest—the position reserved for kings. The legs also were wrapped separately and the feet placed in golden sandals.

The late king's head and neck received special attention. The embalmers were careful that the head retain its shape and that the head and neck be securely fastened to the torso. To help make the head secure, heavy necklaces of gold and jewels were fastened around the neck.

Next, layer after layer of linen strips were wound around the body. Within each layer were more precious ornaments, including amulets and talismans intended to invoke the aid of the gods and to protect Tutankhamen's spirit in the underworld. A golden belt encircled his waist, with a ceremonial dagger to fight off demons.

Finally, the body—now a mummy—was wrapped in a large linen sheet and tied with strong bands. A solid gold mask, an exact likeness of Tutankhamen, was placed carefully over the face. Golden hands holding the crook and flail, symbols of royalty, were sewed onto the shroud.

At each point in the mummification process, priests—some of them wearing masks representing various gods—chanted prayers from the Book of the Dead. When placing a headrest, for instance, the priest intoned, "Awake out of thy sufferings, O thou who liest prostrate. They [the gods] keep watch over thy head in the horizon. Thou art lifted up, thy word is truth in respect of the things which have been done by thee."[6]

Tutankhamen was then returned to the royal palace to lie in state. His widow Ankhesenamen, who had changed her name to conform to the religious change, stood at his feet, playing the part of Isis reciting prayers to restore Osiris to life.

Funeral Procession

After a procession down the Nile to four sacred cities, the mummy was returned to Thebes, to the western bank of the river. After a four-day funeral the body was taken into the sandy, rocky wasteland, subsequently called the Valley of the Kings, for entombment.

Egyptian kings had long since abandoned aboveground tombs such as the enormous pyramids at Giza. While these proclaimed the late ruler's grandeur, they stood as an invitation to robbers who did not fear protective spells and who were willing to risk death by impalement if they were caught. Instead, tombs were underground, carved into rock if possible, and tightly sealed, with memorial temples above.

Even this arrangement, however, proved too vulnerable to robbers, so beginning in about 1491 B.C. with Tutankhamen's ancestor, Thutmose I, royal tombs and chapels were separate. The chapels were built on the edge of the desert across the Nile west of Thebes. The tombs were carved into the rocky cliffs lining the Valley of the Kings.

While Tutankhamen's mummification and funeral had been conducted with all due pomp and dignity, the same probably could not have been said for preparation of the tomb. It was usual for work to begin on a pharaoh's tomb during his lifetime, but apparently no one expected Tutankhamen's life to be so short.

The Tomb

The tomb is small for a royal burial. Its floor space, slightly more than 1,000 square feet, is less than half that of the kings who came before or after. Archaeologists think it might have been intended for something—or someone—else and was hurriedly expanded into something that would barely suit the occasion. Another possibility is that the tomb was indeed intended for Tutankhamen, but that it had to be scaled down and quickly finished in time for the funeral. There was no time even to erase the red chalk marks made by the masons or to sweep up all the limestone chips. In the burial chamber the painted scenes of the afterlife did not have time to dry before the funeral and would be smudged.

Not only did the tomb need to be finished in time for the burial, but it also had to be furnished for everything that the late pharaoh would need in the afterlife. So, in the brief time that would have been available after the masons finished and before the burial, the three rooms other than the burial chamber—the antechamber, annex, and treasury—were packed with jars of food and wine, perfumes, chariots, weapons, ship models, furniture, tools, clothing, and games. In short, the tomb was equipped so that in death Tutankhamen would have the means to enjoy everything he had during his lifetime. There were even more than 400 carved *shabiti* figures representing servants who would relieve the king of any manual labor in the next world.

Last Journey

On the day following the funeral, Tutankhamen's mummy was placed on a bier, or funeral platform, shaped like a lion. It was then pulled with ropes to the tomb by nine noblemen and two officials representing the northern and southern halves of the kingdom. Once at the tomb, the mummy was placed upright. Priests poured water over the mask to symbolize purification. The head priest—Tutankhamen's uncle and successor, Ay—touched the mouth and eyes with a dagger, ceremonially opening them and restoring the king to life.

Before the mummy was taken down to its final resting place, another rite of mourning took place. His widow and other women of the royal family rushed forward to grasp the mummy around the legs, imploring their lord not to leave them. Then, as red clay pots were solemnly broken, symbolizing death, Ankhesenamen chanted,

> I am thy wife, O great one—do not leave me!
> Is it thy good pleasure, O my brother, that I

should go far from thee?
   How can it be that I go away alone?
   I say: "I accompany thee, O thou who didst like
to converse with me,"
   But thou remainest silent and speakest not.

The court women then replied,
   Alas, alas!
   Raise, raise ceaseless laments!
   O, what a downfall!
   Fair traveler departed for the land of eternity,
   Here he is captured!
   Thou who hadst many people,
   Thou art in the earth which loves solitude!
   Thou who didst move thy legs and didst walk,
   Thou art wrapped and firmly bound!
   Thou who hadst many linen garments and didst
like to wear them,
   Thou liest in yesterday's worn linen![7]

Into the Tomb

At last the mummy was carried down the sixteen steps, through the corridor, through the antechamber, and into the burial chamber. After a bouquet of fresh flowers was placed on the mask, possibly by the widow, the first coffin, made of more than 100 pounds of gold, was closed. This coffin was placed inside a second coffin, and the second within a third. All bore a likeness of the former king.

The nested wooden coffins were placed in an ornately carved stone coffin called a sarcophagus. Goddesses were featured at

This coffin of Akhenaton went missing for more than 70 years. In 2002, German officials who recognized Egypt as its owner, returned it.

each corner, spreading their wings as if to protect the occupant. Surrounding the sarcophagus were four nested wooden shrines, all richly decorated with gold leaf.

The burial chamber was barely large enough to hold the shrines and the coffins within it. After the burial a mud-brick wall was built to separate the burial chamber from the antechamber. Once dry, the wall was painted on the inside to match the other antechamber walls, and the ceremonial door was sealed. There were two more doors to be sealed, one between the antechamber and corridor and another between the corridor and staircase. The last of the lights was extinguished, and Tutankhamen was left to what was hoped would be eternal rest.

The Robberies

That rest, however, would not last long. The sealed doors were to prove no deterrent to robbers; there were two break-ins, both about four years after the burial. The first robbery involved only the antechamber. Some of the stolen goods were recovered and replaced. Before the doors were resealed, the corridor was packed with limestone chips to discourage future robbers.

Soon, however, the robbers struck again, this time gaining access to all parts of the tomb. They were quickly caught, perhaps while they were still inside the tomb, and their loot put back. After the corridor was refilled and the doors sealed, the staircase entrance was buried in hopes that the tomb would be forgotten.

And so it was. During construction of the tomb of a later pharaoh, workmen built their huts directly over the buried entrance. Then, about 1000 B.C., a rash of tomb robberies led officials to remove the mummies and most of the treasure from all the tombs in the Valley of the Kings and rebury them in a central location.

One royal tomb, however, was forgotten. The general Horemheb, after he succeeded Ay as pharaoh, set out to eliminate the name of Akhenaton and his family, including Tutankhamen, from all statues and inscriptions. Only a few inscriptions escaped destruction, and Tutankhamen—and his tomb—slowly faded from memory. The young pharaoh rested in his golden coffin out of sight and mind. He would remain so for more than 3,000 years.

CHAPTER 2

Search and Discovery

King Tutankhamen, his tomb, and the supposed curse surrounding them might never have come to light had it not been for the efforts of Carter, who was convinced the tomb existed and had the determination and persistence to find it, and Carnarvon, who had money and patience enough to see the project through. Their partnership would end with the death of one member and the birth of the curse.

Carter received no formal schooling in his native England. Instead, he was taught to draw by his father, an artist who specialized in drawings of animals. In 1890, when he was 17, a neighbor for whom his father had worked recommended him to a professor from Egypt who was looking for someone to help him finish a series of drawings of the inside of ancient tombs. Carter was hired, and three months later he was taken to Egypt by an exploration team as an illustrator.

Carter worked for nine years under some of the world's greatest archaeologists, learning from them and teaching himself about ancient Egyptian culture. He learned so well that in 1899, at the age of 25, he was appointed by Sir Gaston Maspero, head of the Egyptian Antiquities Service, to be its head inspector in the southern part of the country, which included the Valley of the Kings. While working in this post he gradually became convinced, against prevailing opinions, that at least one royal tomb had yet to be discovered—that of Tutankhamen.

Tourists gather at the entrance of King Tut's tomb to wait for their tour to begin.

The Missing Pharaoh

Most archaeologists at the time believed that no more royal mummies were to be found in the Valley of the Kings. The large collection of about 40 such mummies that had been secretly buried by priests thousands of years ago had been found in 1875 by a family that for centuries had made their living robbing tombs. Family members were caught and forced to confess, and authorities recovered the mummies, all neatly labeled by the priests who had buried them. Tutankhamen was not among them.

A few years later five more tombs were discovered. They had been robbed of all treasure, but the mummies—none of them Tutankhamen—had been left behind. Then after a long dry spell, American lawyer and amateur archaeologist Theodore M. Davis found the empty tomb of Horemheb and said, "I fear that the Valley of the Kings is now exhausted."[8]

Carter was not so sure. Horemheb, for reasons that remain unclear, had tried to destroy all evidence of Tutankhamen's reign as well as that of Ay. He sent men throughout Egypt to smash statues and remove any inscriptions referring to his two immediate predecessors, but some survived. In 1907 the French archaeologist Georges Legrain discovered a stele, or pillar, referring to Tutankhamen's coming to the throne. That same year Davis found, in a mostly empty tomb, some gold leaf stamped with Tutankhamen's name. He also found, in a pit near the entrance to the tomb of Ramses II, remnants of pottery, cups, and jars, one of which bore Tutankhamen's name.

Looking Elsewhere

Davis proclaimed that the tomb in which he found the gold foil was that of Tutankhamen. Carter knew better. The tomb was far too small even for the most insignificant of pharaohs. Davis's discoveries, however, convinced him that Tutankhamen's tomb was somewhere in the area.

It would be some time, however, before Carter could begin the search. After offending some drunken but very influential French officials, he had been dismissed from the Antiquities Service in 1903 and spent the next four years guiding tourists and selling a few antiquities he had found or traded for.

Then in 1907 Maspero, who had dismissed Carter only with reluctance, introduced him to George Edward Stanhope Molyneux Herbert, fifth earl of Carnarvon. Carnarvon would provide the most essential ingredient for Carter's searches—money. A major exploratory season, or "dig," involved the hiring of several hundred workers and cost what now would be several hundred thousand dollars.

Carnarvon had the money and also an abiding interest in Egypt. He had more or less drifted through his youth, never achieving much at school, attending Cambridge University two years without graduating, and spending seven years traveling here and there around the world.

In his early thirties he was seriously injured in an automobile accident, as a result of which he would always be in fragile health. It was that fragility that took him in 1903, on the advice of his doctors, to the drier climate of Egypt where he became an enthusiastic but very amateurish archaeologist. After four years he decided he needed professional help and was introduced to Carter.

The Work Begins

Carter and Carnarvon began their work in 1907 but not in the Valley of the Kings. Davis had exclusive rights to dig there and

Hot Work

Egypt, particularly in the years before air conditioning, was a difficult place to work, and one of the most difficult, desolate places in Egypt is the Valley of the Kings. Temperatures in the summer routinely exceed 120°F, and it was for this reason that archaeologists had to work in "seasons" lasting from October until April.

An entry from the journal of archaeologist James Breasted, quoted in *The Murder of Tutankhamen* by Bob Brier, gives some idea of the working conditions: "We are at work at 6:00 A.M., and the sun is long down before we stop. I spent yesterday on a ladder, copying from a glaring wall upon which the sun was beating in full force; and I rose this morning with one eye swollen shut. Even with dark glasses, I sometimes find work on a sunlit wall impossible."

would not relinquish them until 1914. But just as plans for the first dig were well under way, World War I broke out, and it would not be until 1917 that work could begin.

Carter's goal was to find the tomb of Tutankhamen. Because of

Davis's discoveries, he was convinced that it lay in the Valley of the Kings, somewhere within a two-and-one-half-acre triangle. The land area was relatively small but was covered in many places with a yards-thick layer of debris from previous excavations. Carter's plan was to remove the debris and go down to bedrock. Always meticulous, he divided the triangle into grids and began working on them one at a time.

During the first year, while clearing away rubble near the tomb of Ramses VI, he came upon the foundations of what had been a group of huts occupied by the workers on Ramses's tomb. The huts had been built not on bedrock but on top of a layer of limestone boulders. Instead of looking under the huts, however, Carter moved to another grid.

Carter's first season—October to April, the only months cool enough for such work—yielded nothing. Season two brought forth some alabaster jars from other reigns but no sign of Tutankhamen. Seasons three through five, lasting into the spring of 1922, produced no discoveries at all.

Discouraging Times

Carnarvon's patience and money, while not running out, were at least growing thin. The cost of maintaining Highclere, his 36,000-acre estate in England, had skyrocketed, and five years had produced nothing of real value. The tomb of Tutankhamen seemed as far away as ever—almost.

Davis had given the artifacts bearing Tutankhamen's name to Herbert Winlock of the Metropolitan Museum of Art in New York. Examining the cups and jars in 1921, Winlock discovered not only the pharaoh's name but also the seal of the royal necropolis, or city of the dead, signifying the burial of a king. Carter, more convinced than ever that Tutankhamen's tomb had to be in the vicinity, managed to talk Carnarvon into financing one last season.

When Carter arrived in the Valley of the Kings in October 1922, he brought with him, in addition to mounds of equipment and hundreds of workers, a pet canary. The Egyptian workers had never seen such an animal and promptly named it the "Golden Bird" and proclaimed it a sign of good luck.

That good luck occurred almost immediately. Carter began digging on November 1, going back to where the workers' huts had been discovered five years earlier. Three mornings later he arrived at the site to find not the usual hubbub of activity, but silence. The quiet, he later wrote, "made me realize that something out of the ordinary had happened, and I was greeted by the announcement that a step cut in the rock had been discovered underneath the very first hut to be attacked."[9]

Uncovering the Stairway

Carter's team worked steadily through that day and the next until the upper edges of the stairway were exposed. It was clear that they had discovered a tomb, but they could not yet tell whether it was unfinished and never used, finished and used but emptied by robbers, or—by the barest of chances—untouched or only partially robbed.

Carter watched "with ill-suppressed excitement"[10] as the steps were uncovered—one by one—along with the level space in front of them. At the area of the stairway opposite the 12th step was the top of a sealed doorway. Some of the seals bore the sign of the royal necropolis, but there were none indicating who was— or had been—buried inside. Carter knew, however, that it must have been a king or a member of a royal family. He also knew, because of the age of the huts covering the entrance, that the tomb had not been entered since about 1136 B.C.

The temptation to go forward must have been immense, but Carter stopped, electing to wait until Carnarvon could be summoned from England. He sent a telegram: "At last have made wonderful discovery in Valley: a magnificent tomb with seals intact; re-covered same for your arrival. Congratulations."[11]

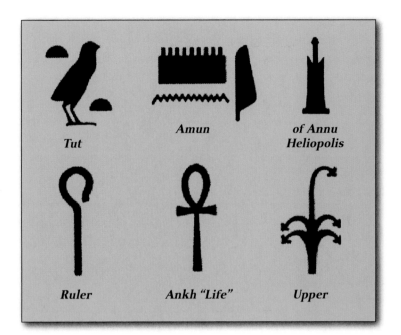

Tut

Amun

of Annu Heliopolis

Ruler

Ankh "Life"

Upper

These hieroglyphics illustrate King Tut's birth name and were found throughout his tomb.

Carnarvon immediately began making preparations for the trip, bringing with him his daughter Evelyn. In the meantime, Carter filled up the stairway, covered the site with boulders, and arranged for trusted guards.

A Cobra's Dinner

When Carnarvon and his daughter arrived in Cairo, Carter was there to meet them. While Carter was gone, an incident occurred that would later become one of the foundations of the King Tut curse.

After the initial discovery Carter had enlisted the aid of Callender, who came to live in Carter's house in Luxor. One afternoon Callender heard a high squeak and a rapid fluttering sound.

He investigated and found the canary in the process of being swallowed by a cobra that had managed to get into its cage.

Winlock later wrote:

> Cobras, as every native knew, grow on the heads of the Old Kings [referring to the cobra on a headdress as a sign of royalty]. The conclusion was obvious. The King's serpent had struck at the mascot who had given away the secret of the tomb [by bringing luck to Carter]. And the sequel was equally obvious . . . that before the winter was out someone would die.[12]

Another version of the event was related by James Breasted, an Egyptologist who later joined Carter's staff. According to Breasted's son and biographer, Charles, his father said that Carter sent a worker to collect something from his house.

> As the man approached the house he heard a faint, almost human cry. Then all was silent again— even the bird had stopped singing. Upon entering, he looked almost instinctively at the cage and saw coiled within it a cobra holding in its mouth the dead canary. News of this spread quickly and all the natives now said: "Alas, that was the King's cobra, revenging itself upon the bird for having betrayed the place of the tomb—and now something terrible will happen."[13]

The curse of King Tut's tomb had claimed its first victim.

The Outer Door

On November 24, with Carnarvon and Evelyn watching, workmen finished clearing the stairway, fully exposing the brick door for the first time. Carter was delighted to see several seals bearing Tutankhamen's name—a certain indication that this was his tomb. Almost immediately, however, came a disappointment. A section of the door was discolored, and it was evident that the doorway had been entered twice and resealed by priests. "The tomb then was not absolutely intact, as we had hoped. Plunderers had entered it more than once," Carter wrote.[14]

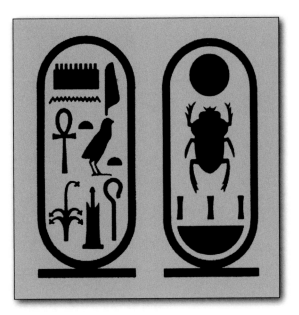

The hieroglyphics on the left illustrate Tut's birth name, and the hieroglyphics on the right illustrate his throne name as the ruler of Egypt.

The fact that the door had been resealed, however, gave Carter hope that perhaps the robbers had been caught and the tomb not totally emptied. He also took comfort in the knowledge that, because the tomb entrance had been completely hidden by the huts, the break-in had to have occurred more than 3,000 years earlier.

Carefully, the bricks making up the door were removed to reveal a 30-foot passageway completely filled with chips of flint. Once this debris was removed, a second door was uncovered, this one, too, showing signs of entry. It was at this point on November 26, the day Carter called "the day of days, the most wonderful that I have ever lived through,"[15] that he made a small hole in the second doorway and peered through to discover that the tomb had not been emptied but, indeed, contained a vast array of priceless objects.

Carter shut and resealed the tomb after only a few days. "The extent of our discovery had taken us by surprise, and we were wholly unprepared to deal with the multitude of objects that lay before us, many in perishable condition and needing careful preservative treatment before they could be touched."[16] As Carter began making preparations, Carnarvon and his daughter returned to England on December 4, planning to return in a few weeks for the opening of the burial chamber.

Work to Be Done

Indeed, many preparations had to be made before work in the tomb could even begin. First, Carter could not hope to deal with the discovery alone and set out to build a team of archaeologists and other experts. Members included archaeologist Arthur C. Mace of the Metropolitan Museum of Art in New York, photographer Harry Burton, Egyptologists Alan Gardiner and James Breasted, and chemist Alfred Lucas. Some of these men would play important roles in the story of King Tut's curse.

The team needed delicate instruments for cleaning and repairing all the various artifacts, along with preservatives and packing materials. They needed a laboratory and a photography darkroom. For the first, they chose the empty tomb of King Seti II, close enough to transport objects and sheltered from the midday sun by overhanging cliffs. The darkroom was set up in another nearby vacant tomb.

When they were ready the team began by emptying the antechamber. They knew the quality of their work would be discussed and critiqued by experts throughout the world and thus were painstakingly careful. There was another reason, Carter wrote, why they felt "a heavy weight of responsibility. Every excavator must, if he have any archaeological conscience at all. The things he finds are not his own property, to treat as he pleases, or neglect as he chooses. They are a direct legacy from the past to the present age, he is but the privileged intermediary through whose hands they come."[17]

Need for Security

Along with the heavy responsibility came a need for security. In addition to the scientific and historical worth of the tomb's treasures, the dollar value was incalculable. Carter needed the tomb guarded round-the-clock by someone he could trust. The man he chose was Richard Adamson, a sergeant in the British embassy's military police.

Carter had originally engaged Adamson to supervise the packing and loading of equipment when he thought his explorations were at an end. His responsibilities changed dramatically with the discovery of the tomb. As night fell on November 4, 1922, the day the steps were discovered, Carter told Adamson, "I am afraid I'll have to ask you to sit out the night on the steps."[18] It would be the first of hundreds of nights Adamson would spend at the site, first outside the steps, later in the antechamber, and finally in the burial chamber itself.

Entry into the burial chamber, however, was still in the future. It would take Carter and his team seven weeks just to clear the antechamber. Every item, no matter how small, had to be photographed where it sat and cataloged before it was moved. And once the time came to move it, extreme care had to be taken that it did not disturb the object next to it.

Some of the objects—jars and stone statues—could simply be picked up and moved. Others, made of perishable material such

This wood-carved mannequin depicts what King Tut may have looked like shortly before his death. It was one of many artifacts found inside his tomb.

as cloth or wood, had to be treated with preservatives before they were moved; otherwise, they might crumble. In addition, some of the larger objects such as chariots and sofas were too large to fit through the passageway. Evidently, they had been assembled inside the tomb and thus had to be disassembled before they could be taken out.

A "Prodigious Task"

The work was hard and dreadfully slow, but Carter thought it was worth the effort. "We have a prodigious task ahead of us," he wrote, "but the results will be gorgeous enough to justify any amount of time."[19]

What made the work even more complicated was the time Carter had to spend away from it because of all the demands made on him. If he had been unprepared for the extent of his discovery, he was even more unprepared for the avalanche of publicity that followed it. "No power on earth could shelter us from the light of publicity that beat down on us," he wrote. "We were helpless, and had to make the best of it."[20]

Tourists descended on the Valley of the Kings in droves, and all wanted to see the inside of the tomb. Very few, mostly fellow archaeologists, got any closer than the entrance. "It was not that we wanted to be secretive, or had any objection to visitors as such—as a matter of fact, there are few things more pleasant than showing one's work to appreciative people," he wrote, "but as the situation developed it became very clear that, unless something was done to discourage it, we should spend the entire season playing showmen, and never get any work done at all."[21]

Waiting and Watching

Even though they were denied entrance to the tomb, visitors nevertheless took up places outside the entrance and all along the path leading to the laboratory. There they would sit—reading, knitting, chatting—all waiting for something to happen, for something to be brought up from the tomb and transported to the laboratory. On many days they waited in vain, but when objects were brought up, as Carter wrote, "books and knitting were thrown aside and the whole battery of cameras was cleared for action and directed at the entrance passage."[22]

Carter did nothing to discourage such activity. Indeed, whenever possible he ordered objects to be carried into the sunlight uncovered so that they could be seen and photographed. Perhaps the most exciting—and just a bit spooky—occurrence of this kind came when it appeared to onlookers that Tutankhamen himself was slowly ascending the 16 steps from his tomb into the sunlight. Actually, the object was a wooden statue of the king that Carter thought must have been used as a mannequin for the person who arranged the pharaoh's wigs.

Carter simply could not, however, refuse all visitors entrance to the tomb. There were fellow archaeologists—he did not mind those—but also Egyptian politicians, British nobility, and museum officials. Many of these he simply could not turn down, much as he might have liked to. "This was a difficulty that came upon us so gradually and insidiously that for a long time we none of us realized what the inevitable result must be," he wrote, "but it brought work practically to a standstill."[23]

The Correspondents

But far worse than the tourists and visitors, in Carter's opinion, were those whom he sarcastically referred to as "our friends the newspaper correspondents, who flocked to The Valley in large numbers and devoted all their social gifts . . . towards dispelling any lingering remains of loneliness or boredom that we might still have left to us."[24] He was relieved when Carnarvon granted exclusive rights for coverage of the tomb and its treasures to the *London Times.* This, however, would enrage other newspapers and, in the end, perhaps create more problems for Carter and Carnarvon than it solved.

The objects from the tomb, once removed to the laboratory, could not simply stay there. They had to be moved to Cairo, there to receive more attention and to be stored and displayed by the Department of Antiquities. The department sent a barge down the Nile to receive the objects, but how were they to be transported from the tomb to the river? Many were too brittle to be carried by camel or even by hand. The solution was a railway, but not one in the usual sense.

Eventually, under temperatures well above 100°F, the precious cargo was loaded on flatbed cars. "We had to lay [the railroad] as we went," Carter wrote, "carrying rails round in a continuous chain as the cars moved forward. Fifty labourers were engaged in this work."[25] Even with so much manpower, the five-and-one-half-mile journey took 15 hours.

Carter and Carnarvon knew that many more years of work lay ahead. Only the antechamber had been emptied. Each of the hundreds of additional items in the tomb would have to be carefully cataloged and, in many cases, painstakingly repaired. Carnarvon was clearly looking forward to the future when he told an interviewer before he left for England, "This [next] part of the tomb [the burial chamber] will take months to examine, and I can only hope that work may be carried on without the constant interruptions which have been the chief feature of this season's campaign."[26]

The work would, indeed, be carried on, but the association between Carnarvon and Carter would last only a few more months, ending in tragedy. And when it ended, the legend of King Tut's curse would begin.

CHAPTER 3

The Legend Begins

When Carnarvon, who had returned to England in early December after the initial discovery of Tutankhamen's tomb, returned to Egypt for the opening of the burial chamber, it might have been with some misgivings. He had been warned that his life might be in danger but chose to ignore the warning. Had he heeded it, he might have lived and the curse of King Tut might never have come to pass.

Carnarvon, like many people in Great Britain at the time, was deeply interested in the occult. He was a member of the London Spiritual Alliance and would sometimes organize séances, small gatherings at which he and guests would try to communicate with a spirit world. Even Carter participated when he was at Highclere in the spring of 1919.

One of the most famous spiritualists in Great Britain was an Irishman, William John Warner, who also styled himself Count

Louis le Warner Hamon or "Cheiro." Among his notable clients who had their palms read and fortunes told were future prime minister Arthur Balfour, author Mark Twain, and even the future King Edward VII of Great Britain.

Whether or not Carnarvon belongs on the list is not certain, but for some reason Cheiro sent the earl a message in December 1922, about one month after the opening of the tomb. He claimed it had been sent to him by the spirit of Meket-aten, a daughter of Akhenaton, and warned Carnarvon against removing any objects from the tomb and that if he did, "he would suffer an injury while in the tomb—a sickness from which he would never recover, and that death would claim him in Egypt."[27]

Velma

Having received the message, Carnarvon reportedly said that he would go ahead with his plans for the tomb no matter what. However, according to the memoirs of his son, shortly to inherit the Carnarvon title, the earl sent for his own spiritualist, a man known only as "Velma."

According to writer Barry Wynne in his book *Behind the Mask of Tutankhamen*, Velma supposedly listened to Carnarvon describe his message from Cheiro and then read his palm, noting some ominous spots near his "life line" and seeing "great peril for you. . . . Most probably—as the indications of occult interest are so strong in your hand—it will arise from such a source."[28] Then, at a second meeting just before Carnarvon left for Egypt, Velma

Tomb curses sometimes invoke the wrath of Thoth, an Egyptian god, upon thieves.

pointed out that one spot "on the Life Line seemed perilously close to the earl's present age."[29]

Velma then was said to have looked into his crystal ball, seeing first an Egyptian temple, then a golden mask being placed over the face of a king, presumably Tutankhamen, and finally the interior of a tomb. Velma said he saw flashes of light from inside the tomb, then images of spirits that "demanded vengeance against the disturbers of the tomb."[30]

When Carnarvon replied that he was determined to return to Egypt to continue working on the tomb, Velma was supposed to have said, "If I were you . . . I should make some public excuse and finish. I can only see disaster to you, without any adequate gain to humanity to justify your sacrifice."[31]

Wynne's account of the exact words used by Velma and Carnarvon cannot be verified, but Carnarvon's son, in his memoirs published in 1976, confirmed that the meetings took place.

Worldwide News

It was not surprising that Carnarvon should have received such warnings. In the first place, the discovery of Tutankhamen's tomb had made the front pages of newspapers around the world. Carnarvon and Carter had become celebrities, and interest in ancient Egypt was higher than it had ever been.

Such interest had been growing, in fact, ever since the translation of the Rosetta Stone in 1922 first made it possible to decipher Egyptian hieroglyphics. The stone was written in three scripts, one being Greek, which enabled it to be translated. Shortly afterward, however, ancient mummies, rather than being regarded in the spiritual sense of having been prepared for an afterlife, had come to be associated with evil.

The first account of a mummy's curse came in a book, *The Mummy*, written for children in 1827 by English author Jane Loudon Webb. In the book, the hero Edric—in much the same way as Mary Shelley's Dr. Frankenstein—brings the mummy of the pharaoh Cheops back to life. At one point, after an electric shock, the mummy's eyes

> had opened . . . and were now fixed on those of Edric, shining with supernatural luster. In vain Edric attempted to rouse himself; —in vain to turn away from that withering glance. The mummy's eyes still pursued him with their ghastly brightness; they seemed to possess the fabled fascination of those of the rattle-snake, and though he shrank from their gaze, they still glared horribly upon him.[32]

More Mummy Tales

Other authors pursued similar themes. An 1828 novel, *The Fruits of Enterprise*, by an anonymous author, had an explorer using ignited parts of mummies as torches. In 1869 Louisa May Alcott wrote a short story, "Lost in a Pyramid," in which a mummified body was used as a torch. Closer in time to the discovery of Tutankhamen's tomb was the 1903 book *The Jewel of Seven Stars* by Bram Stoker, who also wrote *Dracula*. In this book archaeologists ignore a curse carved on a tomb's door and steal a fabulous jewel from a mummy's hand. Later, all who are associated with the jewel begin to die.

Despite all the warnings, Carnarvon returned to Egypt in January 1923 to prepare for the following month's formal opening of the burial chamber. February 17 was selected as the date,

The Rosetta Stone, seen here in the British Museum in London, is a granite slab bearing an inscription that was the key to deciphering Egyptian hieroglyphics.

and rows of chairs were set up in the annex to accommodate a carefully selected audience. Carnarvon and Evelyn were there, of course, as were Callender, Mace, and the rest of the team members. But also on hand were the British high commissioner for Egypt and his wife; the ambassadors from France, Belgium, and the United States; 4 former prime ministers of Egypt; and a host of other dignitaries and visiting archaeologists—more than 40 people in all, not counting the Egyptian workers.

At about two o'clock in the afternoon, the group descended the 16 stairs into the tomb. As they did so, Carnarvon turned back to the watching crowd and joked, "We're going to have a concert! Carter's going to sing a song!" At this, Arthur Weigall, an Egyptologist acting as a correspondent for the *London Daily Mail*, turned to another reporter and said, "If he goes down in that spirit, I give him six weeks to live."[33]

Opening the Chamber

When everyone had been seated or was standing at the back of the antechamber, Carter climbed onto a low platform and began to chip away delicately at the plaster under the wooden lintel of the door into the burial chamber. "It was with a trembling hand that I struck the first blow," he wrote.[34]

When he had opened a large enough hole to admit a flashlight, Carter peered through. After several seconds, during which onlookers were said to have held their breath, he exclaimed, "I see a wall of gold-and-blue faience [highly colored glass]!"[35] He then began widening the hole, carefully prying each stone loose as Mace held it to prevent it falling into the chamber. Once loose, the tile was passed by Mace to Callender to an Egyptian foreman to another worker and finally up the stairs.

When the hole was large enough Carter eased through, followed by Carnarvon and Pierre Lacau, director-general of the Egyptian Antiquities Service. Later that day Carnarvon described the experience to Arthur Merton of the *Times*:

> I find it difficult to describe what I felt when I entered that inner chamber, for of a surety, I never dreamt I should gaze upon the amazing sight which met my eyes. . . . With the greatest care I followed Mr. Carter in and whatever emotion and excitement I may have felt when I entered the first chamber

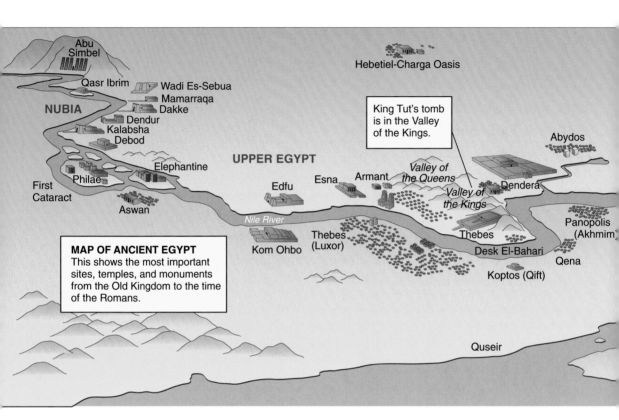

MAP OF ANCIENT EGYPT
This shows the most important sites, temples, and monuments from the Old Kingdom to the time of the Romans.

were as nothing when I was going into what un-doubtedly was the practically untouched tomb.[36]

The Outer Shrine

The first thing the three men saw was that the object Carter had said was a golden wall was not a wall at all but instead the side of an enormous shrine made out of gilded wood. They then discovered that the room, like the antechamber and annex, had been disturbed. Some pieces of jewelry were scattered around the entrance, probably dropped by the robbers in their haste.

The shrine was huge—7 by 11 feet by 9 feet high—filling the entire chamber except for a surrounding space two feet wide. Picking their way carefully, Carter, Carnarvon, and Lacau made

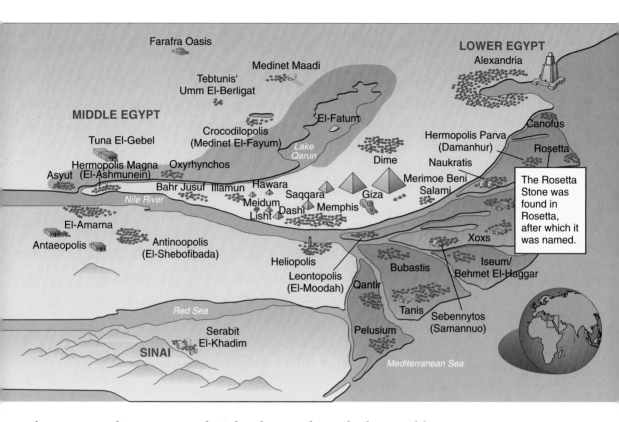

The Rosetta Stone was found in Rosetta, after which it was named.

their way to the eastern end of the shrine where the large folding doors were bolted but not sealed. This, for Carter, was the deciding moment: "Had the thieves penetrated within it and disturbed the royal burial? . . . Eagerly we drew the bolts, swung back the doors, and there within was a second shrine with similar bolted doors, and upon the bolts a seal, intact. This seal we determined not to break, for our doubts were resolved."[37]

Carnarvon knew what this intact seal meant. In a subsequent interview he said, "It was, therefore, almost certain that the body of the King was lying somewhere in this second shrine. As far as I know, this had never happened before. We have only found royal personages either hidden away or very much plundered."[38]

Doing Reverence

Carter wrote that there were two reasons that he did not want to break the inner seal. The first was that he feared it would cause damage to the second shrine, but the second reason was more personal than practical:

> A feeling of intrusion had descended heavily upon us with the opening of the doors, heightened, probably, by the almost painful impressiveness of a linen pall [cloth], decorated with rosettes, which dropped above the inner shrine. We felt that we were in the presence of the dead King and must do him reverence, and in imagination could see the doors of the successive shrines open one after the other till the innermost disclosed the King himself.[39]

Carter and Carnarvon spent about 20 minutes in the burial chamber before emerging to let some of the others come in for a look. Before they left, however, Carter found a small oil lamp whose base bore hieroglyphics, reading, "It is I who hinder the sand from choking the secret chamber. I am for the protection of the deceased."

This, according to Carter, was the first time he or anyone else had been in the burial chamber since the ancient robbery. In his official version he writes that on November 26—his "day of days"—he and the other members of the party only peeked inside the antechamber, after which they "slept but a little, all of us, that night,"[41] wondering what lay inside.

Secret Return

Actually, they slept little because they secretly returned to the tomb—this time without Egyptian inspectors around—to satisfy their curiosity. Not only did they explore the antechamber, but they also very likely entered the burial chamber as well, making a small hole at the base of the door and closing it when they left. Carter never mentioned this nighttime visit in his official writings because it had violated regulations that required representatives of the Egyptian government to be present.

The truth emerged only later and in bits and pieces. Carnarvon wrote in the draft of an article never published that "we enlarged the hole and Mr. Carter managed to scramble in—the chamber is sunk 2 feet below the bottom of the passage—and then, as he moved around with the candle, we knew that we had found something absolutely unique and unprecedented."[42] The official version says the hole was only large enough to look through with the aid of a flashlight.

The truth was also revealed in an obscure journal article by Lucas, who worked with Carter for more than 10 years helping to clear the tomb of its treasures. Writing in 1947, eight years after Carter's death, Lucas said he had suspicions about the hole in the burial chamber door. He wrote:

> Carter's published statement that the hole had been filled up and re-sealed is misleading. The hole, unlike that in the outermost doorway, had not been closed and re-sealed by cemetery officials, but by Mr. Carter. Soon after I commenced work with Mr. Carter [in December 1922] he pointed out to

me the closing and re-sealing, and when I said that it did not look like old work he admitted it was not and that he had done it.[43]

The Cousin's Story

Furthermore, Carnarvon's cousin Mervyn Herbert said that he learned of the episode directly from Carnarvon and his daughter just before the official opening of the burial chamber:

> Porch [Carnarvon's nickname from the title he held, Viscount Porchester, before inheriting the earldom] . . . said that it would really be alright and he could quite well get me in while the tomb was being opened. Then he whispered something to Evelyn and told her to tell me. This she did under the strictest promise of secrecy—it is a thing I would never give away in any case and it is one which I think ought not to be known at any rate not at present. Here is the secret. They had both already been into the second Chamber! After the discovery they had not been able to resist it. They had made a small hole in the wall (which they afterwards filled up again) and climbed through. She described to me very shortly some of the extraordinary wonders I was soon to see.[44]

And so, although it has never been connected to the story of the curse, the fact remains that the initial entry into Tutankhamen's burial place was unauthorized and covered up with a false report.

The formal opening of the burial chamber was finished, but, as distinguished as the audience had been, there was an even more important personage in Luxor, one who merited a private showing. Queen Elizabeth of Belgium, accompanied by her son Prince Alexander, visited the tomb on February 18. The queen and her son, Carter wrote, were "keenly interested in everything they saw."[45] They were so interested, in fact, that they would return three more times within the next week.

The Glittering Serpent

Carter and Carnarvon prepared a special treat for the queen's fourth visit. As she watched, Carter opened one of the sealed boxes that had been found in the treasury. He carefully removed the royal seal—a jackal and nine bound slaves—to reveal a linen-wrapped package. When the wrapping was removed, the queen saw a snake made of gilded wood that had quartz eyes that seemed to flash in the lamplight.

Carter called the snake, symbol of one of the 42 ancient provinces of Egypt, "a true marvel, in style and execution, and a most beautiful piece of naturalistic carving."[46] The Egyptian workmen had other thoughts. To them, this was the cobra that had eaten Carter's Golden Bird, and many saw it as a sign of impending disaster.

On February 26 Carter and Carnarvon closed the tomb for the season, with work scheduled to resume the following fall. Still, however, there was little rest for the archaeologist and his patron. Ever since the discovery, tension had increased between Carter and Carnarvon on one side and Egyptian authorities on the other, the latter fearful that many of Tutankhamen's treasures would be taken away to England.

There was even friction between Carter and Carnarvon. The

two men began to argue over matters such as how to deal with the Egyptian government and with newspaper reporters. It was even rumored that Carnarvon was uneasy at the affection his daughter was displaying for the archaeologist. At one point, when Carnarvon visited Carter in an attempt to iron out their differences, Carter ordered him to leave.

Carnarvon's Troubles

The physical toll taken by the work and heat, the excitement surrounding the opening of the burial chamber, and the stress caused by the various arguments began to affect Carnarvon's health. He grew weak and lost several teeth. He was prone to moody sulks and violent tantrums. He was furious, for instance, at some reporters who—jealous of the exclusive rights given to the *Times*—began to criticize him and Carter for invading the sanctity of the burial chamber, hinting that nothing but evil could come of it. In reply, the *Times* ran an article quoting an "eminent Egyptologist," probably Jean Capart, as saying,

> Some people are seized with pity for the hapless fate of poor King Tutankhamen, who finds himself disturbed in his earthly rest by the curiosity of archaeologists. To hear them, one ought immediately to restore the protective walls behind which he has escaped the seekers for treasure . . . [but] something more than the groans of neurasthenics [people suffering from a psychological disorder] and lunatics is necessary to convince me that the Egyptologists are violating the secret of death in a sacrilegious manner.[47]

Carnarvon's difficulties with Carter were eventually smoothed over, Carnarvon having written a note saying, "Whatever your feelings are or will be for me in the future my affection for you will never change. I'm a man with few friends and whatever happens nothing will ever alter my feelings for you."[48] The quarrel having ended, the English lord and his daughter left Luxor for Cairo in early March. He intended to meet with Lacau about how the tomb's artifacts were to be divided, but the meeting never took place.

The Mosquito Bite

At some point during the time the tomb was being closed for the season, Carnarvon was bitten on the cheek by a mosquito. A few days later, while shaving, he was thought to have nicked the bite with his razor. Although he treated the wound immediately with iodine, infection set in, and he began to suffer from swollen glands and a high fever. Merton of the *Times* would report later that Carnarvon "paid no attention to the bite, and in shaving took off the scab. The minute exposed wound became infected, possibly by dust, but more probably by a fly, and a slight swelling showed itself in one of the glands. Medical aid was sought at Luxor, and when he left for Cairo on March 14 he was decidedly better."[49]

The physician who treated Carnarvon in Luxor was Frank McClanahan, a medical missionary from the United States. In a newspaper article in 1972 he recalled being summoned to the Englishman's hotel. "He was sitting up in bed," McClanahan remembered. "There was a mosquito bite on the side of his forehead. A red streak was running down from it."[50] After treating the spot, McClanahan recommended that Carnarvon remain in bed for several days to give the infection time to heal, but his patient refused and went on to Cairo.

Once there, Carnarvon's condition grew worse. His daughter had tried to keep his illness quiet. She had even written to Carter that her father's meeting with the Antiquities Service had been postponed because its director had the flu. At last, however, on March 18 she wrote to Carter that Carnarvon was so ill he was virtually unable to move.

Carter was alarmed, but another letter then arrived from Albert Lythgoe, Egyptian curator of the Metropolitan Museum of Art. Carnarvon's condition, he reported,

> is a little bit better today—for which we are all thankful. Yesterday was a most anxious time for everyone, but his temperature has lessened today and they apparently feel the trouble is more localized or restricted. We saw Lady Evelyn for a few moments just now in the hall after lunch, and although her anxiety is not as great as yesterday she doesn't feel that the danger is passed by any means.[51]

Urgent Telegram

Evelyn was correct. Shortly after Lythgoe's letter arrived in Luxor, Carter received a telegram from Carnarvon's private secretary, Richard Bethell, reading, "I'm sorry to tell you that C. [Carnarvon] is seriously ill. Eve [Evelyn] does not want it known how bad he is, but that poisoned bite has spread all over him and he has got blood poisoning. . . . There is hope that he may throw it off in a day or two, but otherwise I am afraid it looks pretty serious."[52]

He did not throw it off, and Bethell sent Carter a telegram: "Lord Carnarvon gravely ill, high fever."[53] Only then did Carter leave Luxor for Cairo.

Now, as Carnarvon lay ill, an incident occurred that would prove to be the real beginning of the legend of King Tut's curse. One of the books of the highly popular novelist, Marie Corelli, had involved the reincarnation of an ancient Egyptian princess. In early April Corelli, whose real name was Mary Mackay, wrote a letter to the *New York Times* that said,

> I cannot but think some risks are run by breaking into the last rest of a king in Egypt whose tomb is specially and solemnly guarded, and robbing him of his possessions. According to a rare book I possess . . . entitled *The Egyptian History of the Pyramids*, the most dire punishment follows any rash intruder into a sealed tomb. The book . . . names "secret poisons enclosed in boxes in such wise that those who touch them shall not know how they come to suffer." That is why I ask, Was it a mosquito bite that has so seriously infected Lord Carnarvon?[54]

Furthermore, she wrote, this mysterious book, of which no trace has ever been discovered, contained the curse saying that death would come on his wings to anyone disturbing the tomb of a pharaoh.

Death Approaches

Meanwhile, Carnarvon's condition grew worse with each passing day. He evidently knew his death was near. His sister, Lady Burghclere, would write in her memoirs, "Lord Carnarvon was very tired. . . . 'I have heard the call,' he said to a friend. 'I am preparing.'"[55]

A Widow's Tribute

When Tutankhamen's sarcophagus was finally opened and his mummy revealed, a wreath of flowers was found to have been placed on his mask, circling the royal cobra emblem. They were very likely placed there before the lid was lowered by his widow, Ankhesenamun.

Howard Carter wrote, as quoted in Bob Brier's *The Murder of Tutankhamen*, that "perhaps the most touching [object found] by its simplicity was the tiny wreath of flowers . . . around these symbols, as it pleased us to think, the last farewell offering of the widowed girl queen to her husband, the youthful representative of the 'two kingdoms.'"

Carnarvon's son, who had been traveling in India, hurried to his father's side. He later wrote, "When I arrived in Cairo, I drove at once to the Hotel Continental. My father was unconscious. Howard Carter was there, and my mother, Lady Almina. I was awakened during the night. It was ten minutes before two. The nurse came and told me Father had died. My mother was with

This cosmetic jar, made of ivory, calcite, and wood, was one of hundreds of artifacts found in King Tut's tomb.

him. She closed his eyes."[56]

Carnarvon's death took place on April 6. Because of the publicity he had received—and the deluge of publicity about the events surrounding his death—the story would take root and grow that he had not died of natural causes but from the supernatural powers of the pharaoh whose tomb he had violated.

CHAPTER 4

Deaths and More Deaths

Had Lord Carnarvon's death not been accompanied by strange and inexplicable phenomena, any thoughts of a curse might have died with him. But the tales surrounding the death—and the deaths that were to follow—ensured that "King Tut" would always be coupled in the public's mind with mysterious fatalities.

Carnarvon's son, now the sixth earl, reported that at the moment his mother, Lady Almina, closed his father's eyes, "all the lights suddenly went out. We lit candles. I took my father's hand and prayed."[57]

Some later accounts maintained that the power failure affected only the hotel and not all of Cairo. Carnarvon's son, however, spoke the following day with the head of the Cairo Electricity Board, who told him that a citywide blackout had been reported to him at 2:00 A.M. "'I threw on some clothes and had just got

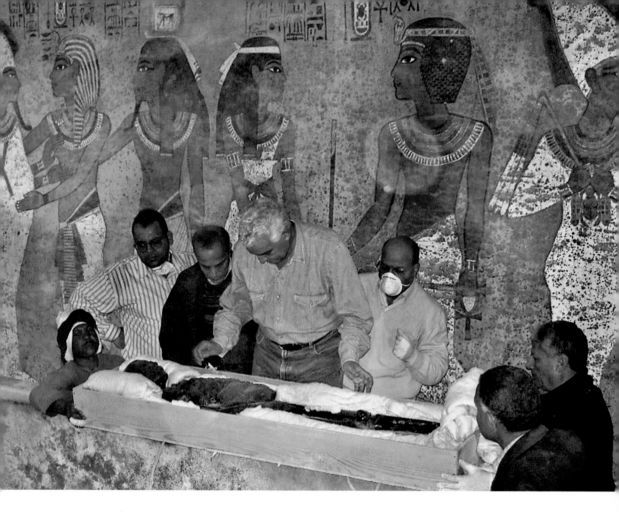

into my car when, to my surprise, all the lights in Cairo went on again," the new earl reported the official as saying. "[Other officials] told me they could not find any reason for this failure and there is no technical explanation for it whatsoever."[58]

The Cairo newspapers had an explanation for the blackout, one that angered Carter. He said, according to Carnarvon's son,

> Well, the newspapers have concocted a story that the lights were put out by the express command of King Tut. They say, in effect, that your father, an infidel, had ignored all the warnings and disturbed the sacred remains of King

Egyptian scientists and workers remove King Tut's mummy from his tomb to prepare it for CT scans, something that was previously not done.

Tutankhamen. To uphold his sovereignty, the King has taken his vengeance and, in order that all should note his displeasure, he turned out every single light in the city of Cairo the moment your father passed away.[59]

Another story making the rounds was that Carnarvon, in his fevered delirium, had kept repeating that a bird was scratching his face. This was later linked to two known curses. Of the first, Ali Hassan, former head of Egypt's Supreme Council of Antiquities, said: "This sentence is of particular interest because something similar appears in a curse-text from [about 2100 B.C.], which says that the Nekhbet bird [vulture] shall scratch the face of anyone who does anything to a tomb."[60] The second, found on the wall of the tomb of Harkhuf at Aswan, reads, "As for any man who shall enter into this tomb . . . I will pounce upon him as on a bird; he shall be judged for it by the great god."[61]

The Dog's Death

There was yet another story to come. "Father died shortly before two o'clock Cairo time," Carnarvon's son told writer Philipp Vandenberg. "As I learned later, something very strange happened here in Highclere [in England] about the same time, shortly before four A.M. London time. Our fox terrier bitch, who had lost her front paw in an accident in 1919 and whom Father loved very much, suddenly began to howl, sat up on her hind legs, and fell over dead."[62]

Either the new earl got his times confused or the dog did not die at the same time as her master. Two o'clock in the morning in Cairo would have been midnight in London, not 4:00 A.M. News-

Did You Know?

Lord Carnarvon's son reported that at the same moment his mother closed the eyes of his dead father, all the lights in the hotel suddenly went out. The head of the Cairo Electricity Board said that a citywide blackout had been reported to him.

paper accounts of the dog's death, however, either ignored the error or shrugged it off. It was too sensational to pass up and fit perfectly into what was now a rapidly growing account of a curse.

The public, in fact, eagerly snapped up all details of Carnarvon's death and the curse that supposedly had caused it, and they were hungry for more. Journalists did their best to feed that hunger, even if it meant a drastic stretching of the truth. For instance, it had been reported the previous year that Carter had found a lamp with the inscription, "It is I who hinder the sand from choking the secret chamber. I am for the protection of the deceased." Now, after Carnarvon's death, the inscription was transferred from a lamp to a statue of the jackal-headed god Anubis and a sentence was added: "and I will kill all those who cross this threshold into the sacred precincts of the Royal King who lives forever."[63]

Sudden Panic

Such reports frightened some people who had bought souvenir items in Egypt that supposedly had been in tombs, especially anything to do with mummies. London's *Daily Express* reported, "The death of Lord Carnarvon has been followed by a panic among collectors of Egyptian antiques. All over the country people are sending their treasures to the British Museum, anxious to get rid of them because of the superstition that Lord Carnarvon was killed by the 'ka' or double of the soul of Tutankhamun."[64]

Reporters also reprinted Corelli's earlier letter in which she claimed to have an ancient book warning that death would come on wings to anyone disturbing the tomb of a pharaoh. To make the story more sensational, some accounts said that instead of being found in a book, the curse was found on a tablet inside Tutankhamen's tomb.

This version of the curse found its way from the newspapers of the day into several otherwise accurate accounts of Carnarvon's death and those of others. It is, however, very likely untrue. Neither Carter nor anyone else connected with Tutankhamen's tomb ever mentioned such a curse on a tablet or anywhere else. It was not listed among the hundreds of objects found in the tomb, nor was a photograph of it ever discovered. Some writers, such as Vandenberg, explain this absence of documentation by alleging that Carter suppressed the finding of the curse, not wishing to start a panic among his Egyptian workers. It is difficult to believe, however, that so meticulous an archaeologist as Carter would use such a subterfuge.

Carter's Strategy

Nevertheless, the story persisted that some sort of curse had been found in Tutankhamen's tomb. Probably one reason is that Carter, although he always said he thought the idea of a curse was nonsense, never denied having found one. Why? Adamson provided the answer. He said years later that as word of the discovery spread—and with it the rumor of a curse—Carter deliberately chose not to deny it. According to Adamson, Carter said, "It will do wonders for security if this [the rumor] gets around."[65]

It was probably inevitable that such a rumor would get started, given the large number of archaeologists who had died, sometimes under mysterious circumstances, after or during explorations in Egypt. In his book *The Curse of the Pharaohs* Vandenberg recounts several such deaths. One of the first was Jean-François Champollion, the man who used the Rosetta Stone

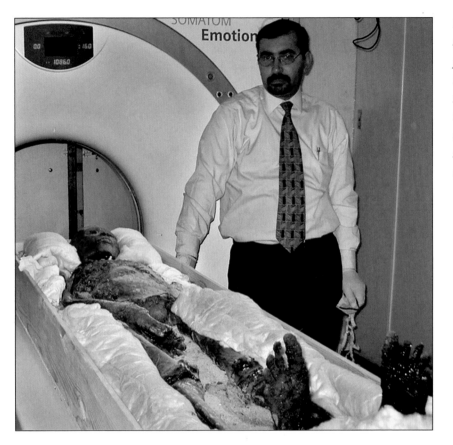

to first translate hieroglyphics. After making his great discovery, his dream of being assigned to Egypt was finally realized when he was 37 years old. He died only five years later from some sort of paralysis.

Likewise, there was Theodor Bilharz, a German anthropologist who had a great interest in the autopsies of mummies. In 1858 he was named a vice president of the Egyptian Society, and one of his duties was to escort the wife of a visiting duke to the Valley of the Kings. While returning to Cairo he suffered feverish cramps. Two weeks later he died at the age of 37.

Closer to the time of the discovery of Tutankhamen, Georg Möller, an expert in Egyptian burial rites, became the scientific attaché at the German consulate in Cairo when he was only 28. He died of a sudden fever while returning to Germany from Egypt in 1921. He was only 44 years old.

Other Incidents

Not all of the cases on Vandenberg's list involve deaths. He writes that at least two prominent Egyptologists—Heinrich Brugsch and Johannes Dümichel—suffered mental problems. Although Vanderberg does not attribute any of the deaths or other problems to a curse, he leaves the question open. In discussing Brugsch's erratic behavior, for example, he writes, "This giant of a man who could forget the world around him when on the trail of a historical problem . . . was he, too, a victim of the curse of the pharaohs?"[66]

In fact, curses on or in Egyptian tombs were rare. The earliest is thought to have been one on a Third Dynasty tomb of about 2600 B.C., reading,

> As for anyone who shall lay a finger on this pyramid and this temple which belong to me and my *ka*, he will have laid his finger on the Mansion of Horus in the firmament, he will have offended the Lady of the Mansion . . . his affair will be judged by the Ennead and he will be nowhere and his house will be nowhere; he will be one proscribed, one who eats himself.[67]

And about 200 years later, in a Fifth Dynasty tomb was this admonition: "As for any people who shall take possession of this tomb as their mortuary property or shall do any evil thing to it, judgment shall be had with them for it by the Great God."[68]

Such curses have never been found on tombs such as Tutankhamen's, those of the Eighteenth Dynasty and later that were meant to be hidden. Rather, they were on tombs or in tomb chapels that were meant to be visited, and the curse was generally a warning against removing any offerings that had been brought to honor the deceased person. A Twelfth Dynasty inscription, for instance, warns that anyone:

> who shall take [the offering] from the statue, his arm shall be cut off like that of this bull, his neck shall be twisted off like that of a bird, his office shall not exist, the position of his son shall not exist, his house shall not exist in Nubia, his tomb shall not exist in the necropolis, his god shall not accept his white bread, his flesh shall belong to the fire, his children shall belong to the fire, his corpse shall not be to the ground, I shall be against him as a crocodile on the water, as a serpent on earth, and as an enemy in the necropolis.[69]

Arthur Conan Doyle's Opinion

Archaeologists might protest that the curse stories coming after Carnarvon's death were nonsense, but their opinions did not seem to count for as much with the public as that of Arthur Conan Doyle. Doyle, the creator of the fictional detective Sherlock Holmes, was known to have an interest in the supernatural. After Carnarvon's death, a *London Times* reporter interviewing the author asked if he thought a curse could have been responsible. Doyle admitted the possibility.

From then on, journalists pounced on the death of anyone even remotely connected with Tutankhamen's tomb, especially when the death had mysterious overtones. One of the first to die, and one of the most prominent, was George Jay Gould, the fabulously wealthy railroad executive. He visited the tomb shortly after Carnarvon's death in April, contracted a fever, and died that May.

The next death was that of Hugh Evelyn-White, an eminent English archaeologist who had done extensive explorations in Egypt and Greece. Although he visited Tutankhamen's tomb, he does not seem to have taken part in the project and was not present at the opening of the burial chamber. Nevertheless, in 1924 he hanged himself, leaving a letter that supposedly read, in part, "I have succumbed to a curse which forces me to disappear."[70]

More Deaths

Two years later George Benedite, a representative from the Louvre museum in Paris, died shortly after visiting the tomb. Differing versions of his death give the cause as either heat stroke or a fall. One account goes so far as to say he fell down the stairs of the tomb.

The same year, 1926, saw at least two more deaths. Archibald Douglas Reed, an English scientist employed by the Egyptian government, was in charge of taking X-rays of Tutankhamen's mummy before it was removed to the Museum of Cairo. Here, once more, accounts of his death differ. One version says that he became ill the day after examining the mummy and died three days later. Another says that his death came in 1924, two years before the mummy was removed.

Aaron Ember, a professor of Egyptology at Johns Hopkins University in Baltimore, Maryland, also died in 1926. When a fire broke out at his home, he escaped but then was burned to death when he ran back inside to save a manuscript, supposedly the Egyptian Book of the Dead. Although Ember had no connection with Tutankhamen's tomb, newspapers linked his death to the curse.

Mace, who was intimately associated with the project, died in 1928. One of the first scientists recruited by Carter after the initial discovery of the tomb, Mace worked alongside Carter for six years and was coauthor with Carter on the first of a three-volume work about the tomb. According to Vandenberg, he complained of increasing weakness and eventually died in the same Cairo hotel as had Carnarvon.

These items, re-creations of clothes found in King Tut's tomb, are on display at a museum in Sweden.

The Bethell Case

Perhaps the most unusual train of events connected with King Tut's curse occurred in 1929. As Carnarvon's private secretary, Bethell was also present at the opening of the burial chamber in 1923. Although some sources place his death much earlier, it was six years after Carnarvon's death that Bethell was found dead in his bedroom—apparently of heart failure. He was only 35 years old.

Shortly afterward, Bethell's father, Lord Westbury, committed suicide by jumping from a building. He left a note reading,

"I really cannot stand any more horror and hardly see what good I am going to do here, so I am making my exit."[71]

Journalists immediately made the most of the story. The United News Service reported:

> The seventy-eight-year old . . . had been worried about the death of his son, which occurred suddenly last November. Rumor attributed the young Bethell's death to the superstition which declares that those who violate the tomb will come to a violent end. Lord Westbury was frequently heard to mutter, "The curse of the pharaohs" as though this had preyed on his mind. [72]

But the story was not over yet. As Westbury's body was being transported, the hearse carrying it struck and killed an eight-year-old boy, Joseph Greer. Newspapers promptly claimed that the curse had claimed another victim, and the furor grew when later the same year Carnarvon's widow, Almina, died of what might have been an infection from an insect bite, much like her late husband.

Weigall and Lythgoe

The press had another field day in 1934. First, in January, Weigall, the Egyptologist/newspaper reporter who had visited Tutankhamen's tomb, died of an undisclosed illness. Newspapers duly linked him with Tutankhamen, even though he had not been part of the expedition. Later that month Lythgoe, another veteran of the opening of the burial chamber, fell ill and speculation about the curse reached new heights.

The furor convinced Winlock to speak out about the curse, something he had previously refused to do. He called a press conference and pointed out, first, that the principal discoverer, Carter, was still alive and that of the approximately 40 people present at either the opening of the burial chamber or of the sarcophagus, only 6 had died and that their average age was almost 60.

Furthermore, he told reporters, he had personally read every hieroglyphic within the tomb and there had not been any curse. Finally, he said, samples taken of air in the tomb and on the surface of the mummy showed no sign of bacteria. Winlock's comments were duly reported, but when Lythgoe died four days later the story of the curse came out just as strong as before.

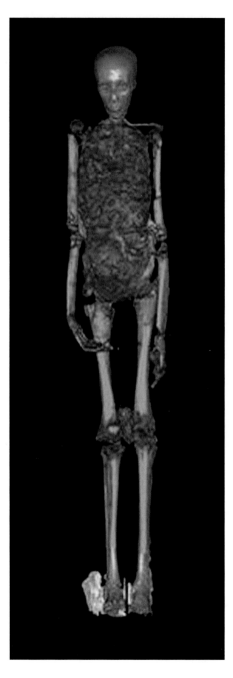

This picture, released by the Egyptian antiquities authority showing a CT scan done on King Tut's mummy, indicates he was not murdered, but may have suffered a badly broken leg shortly before his death.

That story would find new life three years later, when in 1939 Carter, Callender, and Burton all died. The facts that Burton was 61 years old and Carter 66 did not hinder any mentions of the curse. Callender's age at death is unknown.

More Recent Cases

The curse, if some accounts are to be believed, even reached out in more modern times, bringing about the deaths of people who might not even have been born when the tomb was discovered. In 1966 Mohammed Ibrahim, director-general of Egypt's Department of An-

This shabti of King Tut is on display in the "Tutankham and the Golden Age of Pharaohs" exhibit. It is a gilded and painted wooden carving.

tiquities, argued against sending some of the artifacts from the tomb to Paris for an exhibition. Shortly after changing his mind, he was killed in an automobile accident.

His successor, Gamal Mehrez, fared no better in 1972 when a collection of Tutankhamen's treasures were being prepared for shipment to London for an exhibit marking the fiftieth anniversary of the discovery of the tomb. Asked in an interview with Vandenberg if he thought the curse existed, he answered, "If you

Tomb Robbers' Fate

Whether or not people who "violate" Egyptian tombs are subject to a curse is a matter for conjecture, but it is certain that those caught doing so in ancient times faced dire punishment. Records exist of the trial of those who robbed the tomb of King Sobkemsaf I in about 1650 B.C. In a detailed confession, some of which is quoted in *Death and Burial in Ancient Egypt* by Salima Ikram, they told how they "opened their sarcophagi and their coffins in which they were, and found the noble mummy of this king [and his wife]."

For this crime more than 40 people were arrested, tortured, and tried. The punishment for those convicted were to have their eyes put out, their noses and ears cut off, and be put to death by impalement on a sharpened stake. Furthermore, their names were erased, ending their chances for an afterlife.

add up all these mysterious deaths, you might well think so. But I simply don't believe in it. Look at me. I've been involved with

"QUOTE"

"It will do wonders for security if this [rumor of a curse] gets around."

— Carter said this as word of a curse spread; he knew it would keep some from attempting to enter the tomb.

tombs and mummies of the pharaohs all my life. I'm living proof it was all coincidence."[73] Four weeks later Mehrez died of what was diagnosed as a circulatory collapse at the age of 52. He died on the same day as the golden mask that had covered Tutankhamen's face was packed for shipping.

Another story concerns that same shipment of tomb treasures to England. On the airplane, the Royal Air Force *Britannia*, one of the crew members kicked the crate containing the royal mask as a joke, claiming he had just kicked the world's most valuable object. Later, he is supposed to have broken that same leg. Other crew members are later said to have blamed the curse for a divorce and two heart attacks.

Carter's Opinion

Mehrez was by no means alone in dismissing the possibility that a curse had somehow been placed on those involved with the "violation" of Tutankhamen's tomb. Carter, especially, detested all mention of the curse as diminishing the true importance of his discovery, considered perhaps the greatest in the history of archaeology. He said,

> It has been stated in some quarters that there are actual physical dangers hidden in [Tutankhamen's] tomb—mysterious forces, called into being by some malefic power, to take vengeance on whom-

soever should dare to pass its portals. . . . All sane people should dismiss such inventions with contempt. In fact, there is no place less morbid than an Egyptian tomb. The paintings and inscriptions contain not curses on possible intruders but blessings on the deceased, magical spells to ensure a good afterlife.[74]

But if there is no curse at work, how can all the deaths be explained? Some people maintain that it is mere coincidence, but others seek answers in both the natural and supernatural realms. Still others do not know what to believe, but choose to play it safe. Carnarvon's son, interviewed by NBC Television in 1977, said he "neither believed it [the curse] or disbelieved it," but he added later that he would "not accept a million pounds [about $1.9 million) to enter the tomb of Tutankhamun in the Valley of the Kings."[75]

And even Carter, despite his public comments, might have had some misgivings. The unpublished memoirs of Thomas Cecil Rapp, who was a British diplomat in Egypt at the time, state that "[Carter] was suffering too from a superstitious feeling that Lord Carnarvon's death was possible nemesis for disturbing the sleep of the dead, a nemesis that might also extend to him."[76]

CHAPTER 5

Magic or . . . What?

For more than 80 years the Curse of King Tut has seized imaginations, fueled controversy, and sparked numerous scientific investigations. When all has been said and all has been studied, however, we are perhaps no nearer to answering the central questions: Has a curse been at work, reaching across thousands of years to strike down people associated, in however slight a manner, with the opening of Tutankhamen's tomb? And, if a curse has not been at the bottom of the deaths of Carnarvon and others, what has?

People today, even those who contribute to the many Internet sites that deal with the supernatural or paranormal, are reluctant to say they actually believe in the power of the curse. And yet they admit the possibility. An unsigned article on the Web site *KingTutOne.com* ends by saying, "It all really boils down to one question. Do you believe in the curse of the mummy? We leave

The inside of this coffinette, containing some of King Tut's organs, is covered with spells from The Book of the Dead *on the inside.*

that for you to decide."[77] And another unsigned article on the Midnight Fire site recounts some of the deaths and adds, "And there's more, much, much more. One death, even two or three or five or six might have been a coincidence, or a chain of coincidences, but all this (and more, much, much more)? Never. That, to me is a far too far-fetched explanation."[78]

The Role of Magic

The ancient Egyptians would have had no difficulty at all in stating a firm belief in the curse. Magic was an important and integral part of their lives. The Egyptians considered magic, or *heka*, the controlling force for both the world they knew and the underworld where they believed their spirits would go after death. Everyone—people and gods—and everything, no matter how insignificant, was thought to have this force to some degree.

Magical forces, it was believed, could be made to work in a wide variety of ways both positive (healing or protecting) and negative (injuring or destroying). But in order to be put to use, magic needed to be somehow activated, and the most effective way to do so was to employ a spell, either written or—even more powerful—spoken.

Thus it was that objects in Tutankhamen's tomb had not been simply placed there, but had been done so with the proper spell spoken by a priest. Such objects included at least 25 figures of gods, some of whom were unfamiliar to Carter, who wrote, "These comparatively inartistic figures of strange gods are valuable to us as a record of myths and beliefs, ritual and custom, associated with the dead. That they were supposed to be potent for good or evil, or have some form of magic inherent in them, is evident, although their exact meaning in this burial is not clear to us."[79]

"Magical Objects"

The tomb also contained numerous other artifacts labeled "magical objects" by Egyptologist Nicholas Reeves. These included shrines, carved figures, oars, inscribed bricks, and fetishes—small carvings of animals or supernatural figures that were supposed

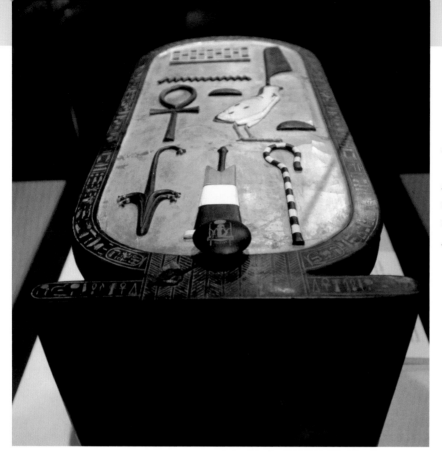

This wooden box found in Tut's tomb, is inscripted with the symbols that represent his birth name.

to have magical powers. The archaeologists knew the significance of some of these objects, such as the oars the dead pharaoh would need to ferry himself through the underworld. But Reeves writes that of others, "Their form is frequently as obscure as their significance."[80]

Tutankhamen's body itself was protected by amulets, more than 140 of them placed within the linen wrappings. These took various shapes depending on what spirit was invoked or from what the king was supposed to be protected. They tended to be much more elaborate than fetishes and were often made of precious metals and jewels. In their book on Egyptian funeral practices, Salima Ikram and Aidan Dodson write, "The power inherent in an amulet was transmitted not only by its shape, but also by its material and colour, all of which helped to endow the wearer with power, protection, and special capabilities."[81]

So it was that magic was an important part of any Egyptian burial and that such magic was particularly potent in the burial of a king. It was believed that the dead ruler needed special protection because, according to Egyptian religion, he would become the god Osiris. Such a curse as the one involving death's wings, if indeed it existed, would have been especially effective when placed in Tutankhamen's tomb.

No Evidence

There are two problems, however, with the curse supposedly found in the tomb. First, there is no reliable evidence that it ever existed. Second, it is not typical of the handful of curses that have been found in tombs, most of which are very specific as to what punishment awaits the interloper. For instance, the curse on the tomb of an overseer named Petety reads, "Listen all of you! The priest of Hathor will beat twice any one of you who enters this tomb or does harm to it. The gods will confront him because I am honored by his Lord. The gods will not allow anything to happen to me. Anyone who does anything bad to my tomb, then (the) crocodile, (the) hippopotamus, and the lion will eat him."[82]

Yet, wings of death or no wings of death, Tutankhamen and his tomb were well protected from a magical point of view. After all, it was his mummy and tomb that survived intact to a greater extent than any other in the Valley of the Kings. Combine this fact with the deaths that occurred after the tomb was discovered, and those who believe in the power of the supernatural could draw the conclusion that a curse was at work.

In our modern society, however, belief in supernatural curses is not as prevalent as in ancient times, and most people tend to look for rational explanations. Such possible explanations have included poisons—either occurring naturally or deliberately placed in the tomb—deadly bacteria, mold spores, and even radioactivity.

It is not as if Carter and his team were unaware that there was some potential danger in opening a burial chamber that had been sealed for more than 3,000 years. Within the limits of the scientific knowledge of the time, they were very careful. On the day after the opening of the burial chamber Lucas, the team chemist, used cotton swabs to take samples from the walls and the bottom of the outer shrine. The result, Carter wrote, was that

> out of five swabs from which cultures were taken, four were sterile and the fifth contained a few organisms that were undoubtedly air-infections unavoidably introduced during the opening of the doorway and the subsequent inspection of the chamber, and not belonging to the tomb, and it may be accepted that no bacterial life whatsoever was present. The danger, therefore, to those working in the tomb from disease germs, against which they have been so frequently warned, is non-existent.[83]

Fungus in the Tomb

While Lucas found no bacteria, he did, however, find a considerable amount of fungus growing on the burial chamber walls. This fungus, he wrote, was "so plentiful as to cause great disfigurement, and they occur also, though only to a slight extent, on the walls of the Antechamber and on the outside of the sar-

cophagus, but in every instance the fungus is dry and apparently dead."[84]

Apparently dead, perhaps, but possibly not. In a news conference in 1962 biologist Ezzedin Taha of the University of Cairo said that he had found the cause of so many early deaths among people who worked with mummies or with artifacts from within tombs. Taha conducted tests on several archaeologists and museum workers and found that many of them had experienced fever and respiratory difficulties from a fungal infection.

Taha concluded that fungus causing this infection was the same one that caused "Coptic itch"—a condition marked by skin rash and respiratory problems that often occurred among people who handled ancient Egyptian documents. He also said that the likely cause was the fungus *Aspergillus niger* and added that, in his opinion, the fungus could have survived during the millennia the tomb was sealed. He said,

> This discovery has once and for all destroyed the superstition that explorers who worked in ancient tombs died as a result of some kind of curse. They were victims of morbific [disease-causing] agents encountered at work. Some people may still believe that the curse of the pharaohs can be attributed to some supernatural powers, but that belongs to the realm of fairy tales.[85]

Taha's Fate

Strangely enough, however, Taha was soon to fall victim, some said, to King Tut's curse. He suffered what possibly was an aneurysm, or burst blood vessel, while driving. His car veered into the path of an oncoming vehicle, and he and two assistants were killed.

In the 1990s Italian researcher Nicoloa Di Paolo identified another fungus—*Aspergillus ochraceus*—at archaeological sites in Egypt. He suggested that breathing air in tombs or handling artifacts taken from them might cause illness. In no cases, however, was *Aspergillus ochraceus* shown to cause a fatal disease.

The same, however, could not be said for yet another fungus. In 1993 German biochemist Christian Hradecky examined the surface of several mummies and found evidence of *Aspergillus flavus*. He found the same fungus in long-rotted food left as offerings in tombs. *Aspergillus flavus* is capable of producing a substance known as aflatoxin, known to be able to cause cancer. Cancer, however, was not among the causes of death of those connected with King Tut's curse.

This gold mask, found on King Tut's mummy, is perhaps the most valuable artifact recovered from his tomb.

Certainly, as they decayed, food, plants, and any other natural substances—including the mummies themselves—would have furnished sources in which fungi could grow. "When you think of Egyptian tombs, you have not only dead bodies but foodstuffs—meats, vegetables, and fruits" intended for the journey to the underworld, said Jennifer Wegner, an Egyptologist at the University of Pennsylvania Museum in Philadelphia. "It certainly may have attracted insects, molds, [bacteria], and those kinds of things. The raw material would have been there thousands of years ago."[86]

Aspergillus flavus and several other potentially harmful mold spores were found on mummies in 1999 by another German, microbiologist Gotthard Kramer. He theorized that when a long-sealed tomb is opened, the first gusts of air might whisk the fungus spores from the surfaces of walls and objects into the air. Then, he said, "When spores enter the body through the nose, mouth or eye mucous membranes, they can lead to organ failure or even death, particularly in individuals with weakened immune systems."[87]

The Anthrax Theory

In 2002 French scientist Sylvain Gandon suggested that Carnarvon's death could have been caused by "infection with a highly virulent very long-lived pathogen" such as *Bacillus anthracis*, cause of the deadly disease anthrax. Canadian doctor James McSherry agreed, saying, "A malignant pustule in the oropharyngeal area [the mouth and throat] would well produce an illness similar to the tragic event that caused Lord Carnarvon's demise." He added,

> Anthrax certainly existed in ancient times and is often assumed to have been responsible for the fifth and sixth plagues of Egypt [livestock disease and incurable skin boils], which are well described in chapter nine of Exodus [in the Bible]. Anthrax spores could have well been present in the tomb, and there would have been a real risk of exposure once the ancient dust was stirred.[88]

Anthrax, however, is almost 100 percent fatal, and it would have been strange if Carnarvon were the only person affected.

Some have wondered if a deadly fungus could have come not from rotten foodstuffs but from a living organism. In his book *The Curse of the Pharaohs* Vandenberg reviews the case of John Wiles, a South African geologist who in 1956 was exploring caves in Rhodesia when he was suddenly surrounded by a swarm of bats. Shortly thereafter he became ill, complaining of aching, fever, and indigestion.

At first doctors thought Wiles had contracted pleurisy, an inflammation of the membrane surrounding the lung and chest cavity. When he did not respond to treatment, he was transferred to another hospital where his condition was determined to be histoplasmosis, a deadly disease transmitted by a fungus growing in bat droppings.

One of the doctors treating Wiles suggested that a similar fungus, perhaps in the droppings of a rodent who had somehow entered the tomb, had been responsible for Carnarvon's death. However, no trace of a rodent or any other animal was reported to have been found in Tutankhamen's tomb.

Hookworms

What if, however, the animal was so small as to escape notice? Vandenberg points to the hookworm as a possible cause of diseases such as those experienced by archaeologists in Egypt. This condition first came to the attention of doctors during the construction of the Gotthard Tunnel, a railway tunnel in Switzerland. Similar symptoms—weakness and anemia, or a deficiency of oxygen in the blood—had occurred in miners in France and Belgium where it was called "miners anemia."

Curse Still Alive

As recently as 2006 the Curse of King Tut's Tomb may have struck again. A team of radiologists was studying the pharaoh's mummy in Cairo when all sorts of difficulties arose.

"While performing the CT (computerized tomography) scan, we had several strange occurrences," said Dr. Ashraf Selim of the Kasr Eleini Teaching Hospital. "The electricity suddenly went out, the CT scanner could not be started and a team member became ill. If we weren't scientists, we might have become believers in the Curse of the Pharaohs."

When some of the tunnel workers in Switzerland were transferred to German hospitals, doctors there discovered the eggs of hookworms in the feces of one of the workers. Research subsequently discovered that the hookworm egg, when hatched, produces a larva that can enter the human body through contact with skin. When the mature hookworm latches onto the lining of the small intestine to feed, it secretes poisons that destroy red blood cells, thus producing anemia.

Egyptian documents dating from about 1600 B.C. describe a condition much like that produced by hookworms, and there has been some speculation that the worms might have caused the weakness that preceded Carnarvon's death. The problem with this notion is that hookworm eggs do not survive more than about two weeks after leaving the body. If Carnarvon encountered hookworms, it could not have been within the tomb.

The Case for Poison

Some have speculated that if animals were not the direct cause of what ailed those who entered Tutankhamen's tomb, then perhaps the source might have been poisons derived from animals. Certainly there is no lack of poisonous animals in Egypt, scorpions being the most prominent. Snakes such as the cobra and asp contain deadly poison. So does the white widow spider, and even the lowly toads dwelling along the Nile have been found to produce an array of poisons in glands located in the hump on their ears.

Egypt is also home to the beetle *Lytta vesicatoria*, otherwise known as the Spanish fly. These beetles, when dried and crushed, produce a powder that can cause inflammation if it comes in contact with the skin. If the powder is taken internally, it can cause severe kidney damage. The effects of the powder were described by the Greek physician Hippocrates as far back as 400 B.C. and likely were known to the Egyptians as well.

The Egyptians also knew about poisonous plants. The first pharaoh, Menes, is recorded to have grown poisonous plants, although there is no clue to exactly what they were. Other ancient records, however, document the uses of such substances as opium, hemlock, henbane, and monkshood.

Tourists explore the Valley of the Kings, the traditional burial ground of the Egyptian pharaohs. For protection, tombs were deep underground, carved into rock if possible, and tightly sealed.

Ergot and Arsenic

Ergot was another deadly substance with which the Egyptians were familiar. This fungus, the scientific name for which is *Claviceps*, infects grain and was a source of epidemics throughout history until brought under control in the twentieth century. The fungus produces an alkaloid that, if a sufficient amount is ingested, can cause nausea, a burning sensation in the arms and legs, and a constricting of blood vessels that can lead to strokes or seizures.

Other poisons available in Tutankhamen's time include arsenic, which was also used in making paint, and mercury, whose uses are on record from as long ago as 1500 B.C. The Egyptians also knew how to distill hydrocyanic or "prussic" acid from peach pits. Prussic acid is thought to be one of the ingredients in the mixture used to coat the linen wrappings of mummies in order to better preserve the bodies.

Arsenic, though not necessarily from Tutankhamen's tomb, may have contributed to Mace's death. In 1927 the archaeologist wrote to Lythgoe that he was suffering from fatigue, shortness of breath, and indigestion. He was considering going to a heart specialist, he wrote, but added that his condition was "a heritage of arsenic poisoning."[89]

Such natural poisons as arsenic—if deliberately placed in a tomb by the Egyptians—would not necessarily have to be injected into the body, either through a bite or smeared on the end of some sharply pointed object. Rather, they could infect tomb intruders simply by contact. Vandenberg writes,

> Some poisons need only brush or penetrate the skin to become effective. Used to paint artifacts and walls were such powerful poisons as aconite, arsenic, and conium. None of them lost their potency even when dried. Moreover, it is a safe bet that poisonous gasses and vapors, in precipitated form, were present in the pharaohs' tombs. The precipitation technique was popular in the Middle Ages. . . . Soaking a candle wick in arsenic was one of the simplest methods. Light a candle and the vapors are deadly. . . . In the airtight chambers of a pharaoh's tomb, such vapors could precipitate and never disappear. Did poisonous candles burn in the tombs while workmen sealed the entry?[90]

Furthermore, Vandenberg argues, many poisons available to the ancient Egyptians might have been just as effective in A.D.

1923 as in 1300 B.C. The interior of tombs, buried several feet underground, was relatively cool, largely airtight, and absolutely dark. He writes:

> The shriveling of poisonous glands or the drying up of poisons themselves does not decrease their potency. Not even a marked change in temperature weakens cobra poison; after a fifteen minute exposure to 100-degree-centigrade temperatures, the venom retains full potency. Snake poisons with a protein base, on the other hand, are not as resistant; they lose their effectiveness at 75 to 80 degrees centigrade, as do certain insect poisons. Ultraviolet rays can also neutralize insect poisons, but the pharaohs' tombs, which these rays cannot penetrate, would have made ideal places for storing such poisons and keeping their effectiveness unimpaired.[91]

Radioactivity

Vandenberg also speculates that another kind of poison altogether—radioactivity—could have been behind the illnesses suffered by many of those involved with Tutankhamen's tomb. This idea was advanced in 1949 by Italian physicist Luis Bulgarini, who said, "I believe that the ancient Egyptians understood the laws of atomic decay. Their priests and wise men were familiar with uranium. It is definitely possible that they used radiation in order to protect their holy places."[92]

Bulgarini's idea was based on the fact that some matter occurring in nature, such as uranium, gives off radioactivity. Generally these are isotopes, variations of elements that are unstable because they do not, as do stable elements, have the same number of electrons as protons. The excess energy is given off in the form of radioactivity until stability is reached. How long an isotope is radioactive depends on its half-life, the time it takes for one-half of its mass to decay. These half-lives can be very short (one hour for chlorine) or very long (an estimated 7.5 billion years for uranium-235). If, then, the Egyptians understood the dangers posed by radioactivity and placed radioactive material in tombs, that material could remain active for thousands of years.

"The floors of the tombs could have been covered with uranium or the graves could have been finished with radioactive rock," Bulgarini said. "Such radiation could kill a man today or at least damage his health."[93]

Exposure to radiation could account for at least one aspect of the mystery surrounding Tutankhamen's tomb. In the weeks before his death, Carnarvon was reported to have lost some teeth. Tooth loss is indeed one symptom of radiation sickness, and it can be a sign of mercury poisoning as well. Subsequent tests, however, have found no trace of radiation in the tomb.

No Single Answer

While scientists and others have put forward many theories and ideas as to what factors other than the power of a curse could explain the deaths of people associated with King Tut's tomb, none is conclusive. One difficulty is that these factors—bacteria, poisons, radiation—seem perhaps to have affected some of Carter's team, but not others. If Carnarvon, for instance, suffered from radiation poisoning, others should have as well. It is also hard to understand how deadly bacteria could have attacked Bethell, who spent only a very short time in the tomb, and not affected Adamson, who spent night after night sleeping in the tomb. And then there are the cases of those people whose deaths have been attributed to King Tut's curse but who never went near the tomb—Bethell's father and the boy struck down by the hearse.

Archaeologists admit that there is an element of danger in exploring tombs and ruins simply because of the nature of the work. "An old joke about archaeology is that when you go home after a hard day in the field and blow your nose, you blow out dirt," said Kenneth Feder of Central Connecticut State University. "Clearly you have been breathing it in, and if you have been exposed to mold, spores or fungi that lay dormant in the earth, there is at least a possibility of being exposed to some nasty stuff."[94]

But that possibility, said fellow archaeologist F. de Wolfe Miller of the University of Hawaii at Manoa, is slim. "We don't know of even a single case of either an archaeologist or a tourist experiencing any negative consequences," he said. "Given the sanitary conditions of the time in general, and those within Egypt in particular, Lord Carnarvon would likely have been safer in the tomb than outside."[95]

Question of Coincidence

The chief difficulty encountered by people who believe in King Tut's curse, however, is that it seems to have been highly selective and capricious. If, as suggested, there was a curse promising death to whomever "disturbs the peace of the pharaoh," then why would Carter, the man most responsible for the discovery of Tutankhamen, live 16 more years and die at age 66, at the time considered an advanced age?

And what about Callender, who lived another 16 years; Doug-

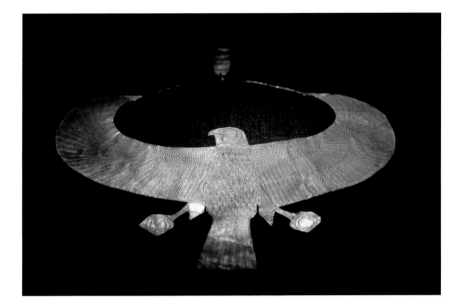

This collar, known as the Falcon Collar, was wrapped around the neck of King Tut's mummy.

las Derry, the scientist who actually dissected Tutankhamen's mummy and died 46 years later at the age of 87; or Lucas, who analyzed tissues taken from the mummy and died 27 years later at the age of 79? Also, what about the person who—if Hoving's account is correct—was the first to disturb the pharaoh's peace—Carnarvon's daughter Evelyn? She died in 1980 at the age of 78. It seems illogical that a curse would ignore these people and bring about the death of an eight-year-old boy in England.

As for Carnarvon, the man whose death ignited the story of King Tut's curse, it is often overlooked that he had been in poor health for many years, really ever since his automobile accident, and that his frail condition had been worsened by stress associated with the tomb and events surrounding it. Weigall, who joked on the day the burial chamber was opened about Carnarvon having six weeks to live, later wrote that "Lord Carnarvon, always a delicate man, looked pale and exhausted as he came up out of the depths; and on the face of all those who had been present there were marks of fatigue and over-excitement."[96]

Updated List

In 1978 stage magician and author James Randi updated a list originally begun by Winlock. The list consisted of 23 people, other than Egyptian workers, most intimately involved with the tomb of Tutankhamen. He found that they had lived an average of more than 24 years after the tomb was opened and had died at an average age of 73.

Dr. Mark Nelson, professor of medicine at Monash University in Australia did a more comprehensive study in 2002. He listed 44 people—all Europeans or Americans—who were in Egypt at the time of the tomb's discovery. Twenty-five were exposed at some point to the tomb or the mummy and might be expected to fall under the curse, and 11 were not exposed. He found no significant difference in the life span of the two groups, and the average age of death in both groups was over 70.

"An Egyptian archaeological dig in the 1920s was inhabited by interesting characters and it was this and the circumstances of the archaeological find of the modern age that has kept the myth of the mummy's curse in the public eye. I found no evidence for its existence," Nelson wrote. "Perhaps finally it, like the tragic boy king Tutankhamen, may be put to rest."[97]

But legends are hard to kill, enduring through the ages much like mummified kings and their tombs. As recently as 2005 a woman in South Africa wrote to Egypt asking if she could give to the government a piece of jewelry she believed came originally from Tutankhamen's tomb. Since she had acquired it, her daughter died of leukemia and her husband also died unexpect-

Groups of tourists stand in front of King Tut's tomb. It is one of the most visited sites in Egypt.

edly, and she was afraid to keep it any longer.

Tutankhamen continues to hold a fascination for all who read about him and the events accompanying the discovery of his tomb. Because of the supposed curse, this obscure boy-king has become the most famous figure in Egyptian history, with the possible exception of Cleopatra. As an anonymous Web site contributor, identified only as Seshat, the ancient goddess of wisdom, wrote,

> The Curse of the Pharaohs is a legend for some and a fact for others; it will always fill the pages of books and the secret corners of our imagination. As we gaze upon the magical inscriptions carved in stone or painted on walls, we are left wondering about the secrets hidden behind their silence. Those magical inscriptions remain a source of mystery to modern spiritualists, as Ra gives birth to another new day above the whispering sands of the Valley of the Kings."[98]

NOTES

Introduction: The Wings of Death

1. Howard Carter and A.C. Mace, *The Discovery of the Tomb of Tutankhamen*. New York: Dover, 1977, p. 96.
2. Quoted in Nicholas Reeves, *The Complete Tutankhamun*. London: Thames and Hudson, 1990, p. 81.
3. Quoted in Philipp Vanderberg, *The Curse of the Pharaohs*. Sevenoaks, UK: Coronet, 1975, p. 19.
4. Quoted in Thomas Hoving, *Tutankhamun: The Untold Story*. New York: Simon and Schuster, 1978, p. 227.

Chapter 1: Prince, King, Mummy

5. Quoted in Christine El Mahdy, *Tutankhamen: The Life and Death of the Boy-King*. New York: St. Martin's, 1999, pp. 318–19.
6. Quoted in E.A. Wallis Budge, trans., "Papyrus of Ani: Egyptian Book of the Dead," University of Pennsylvania African Studies Center. www.africa.upenn.edu.
7. Quoted in Christine Desroches-Noblecourt, *Tutankhamen: Life and Death of a Pharaoh*. London: George Rainbird, 1963, p. 241.

Chapter 2: Search and Discovery

8. Quoted in Reeves, *The Complete Tutankhamun*, p. 38.
9. Carter and Mace, *The Discovery of the Tomb of Tutankhamen*, p. 87.
10. Carter and Mace, *The Discovery of the Tomb of Tutankhamen*, p. 89.
11. Quoted in Hoving, *Tutankhamun: The Untold Story*, p. 81.
12. Quoted in Hoving, *Tutankhamun: The Untold Story*, p. 82.
13. Quoted in Andrew Collins and Chris Ogilvie-Herald, *Tutankhamun: The Exodus Conspiracy*. London: Virgin, 2002, p. 41.
14. Carter and Mace, *The Discovery of the Tomb of Tutankhamen*, p. 92.
15. Carter and Mace, *The Discovery of the Tomb of Tutankhamen*, p. 94.
16. Carter and Mace, *The Discovery of the Tomb of Tutankhamen*, p. 105.
17. Carter and Mace, *The Discovery of the Tomb of Tutankhamen*, p. 124.
18. Quoted in Elaine Edgar, *A Journey Between Souls*. Lafayette, CO: White-Boucke, 1997, p. 38.
19. Carter and Mace, *The Discovery of the Tomb of Tutankhamen*, p. 121.
20. Carter and Mace, *The Discovery of the Tomb of Tutankhamen*, p. 141.
21. Carter and Mace, *The Discovery of the Tomb of Tutankhamen*, p. 143.
22. Carter and Mace, *The Discovery of the Tomb of Tutankhamen*, p. 144.
23. Carter and Mace, *The Discovery of the Tomb of Tutankhamen*, p. 144.
24. Carter and Mace, *The Discovery of the Tomb of Tutankhamen*, p. 142.
25. Carter and Mace, *The Discovery of the Tomb of Tutankhamen*, p. 177.
26. Quoted in Hoving, *Tutankhamun: The Untold Story*, p. 199.

Chapter 3: The Legend Begins

27. Quoted in Collins and Ogilvie-Herald, *Tutankh-*

amun: The Exodus Conspiracy, p. 80.

28. Quoted in Barry Wynne, *Behind the Mask of Tutankhamen.* London: Souvenir, 1972, p. 135.

29. Quoted in Wynne, *Behind the Mask of Tutankhamen*, p. 146.

30. Quoted in Wynne, *Behind the Mask of Tutankhamen*, p. 148.

31. Quoted in Wynne, *Behind the Mask of Tutankhamen*, p. 149.

32. Quoted in Lisa Hopkins, "Jane C. Loudon's *The Mummy!* Mary Shelley Meets George Orwell, and They Go in a Balloon to Egypt." Cardiff School of English, Communication, and Philosophy. www.cf.ac.uk.

33. Quoted in Hoving, *Tutankhamun: The Untold Story*, p. 194.

34. Carter and Mace, *The Discovery of the Tomb of Tutankhamen*, p. 179.

35. Quoted in Hoving, *Tutankhamun: The Untold Story*, p. 195.

36. Quoted in Hoving, *Tutankhamun: The Untold Story*, p. 197.

37. Carter and Mace, *The Discovery of the Tomb of Tutankhamen*, p. 183.

38. Quoted in Hoving, *Tutankhamun: The Untold Story*, p. 197.

39. Carter and Mace, *The Discovery of the Tomb of Tutankhamen*, p. 183.

40. Quoted in Hoving, *Tutankhamun: The Untold Story*, p. 196.

41. Carter and Mace, *The Discovery of the Tomb of Tutankhamen*, p. 101.

42. Quoted in Collins and Ogilvie-Herald, *Tutankhamun: The Exodus Conspiracy*, p. 48.

43. Quoted in Hoving, *Tutankhamun: The Untold Story*, p. 106.

44. Quoted in Collins and Ogilvie-Herald, *Tutankhamun: The Exodus Conspiracy*, p. 51–52.

45. Carter and Mace, *The Discovery of the Tomb of Tutankamen*, p. 186.

46. Quoted in Hoving, *Tutankhamun: The Untold Story*, p. 204.

47. Quoted in Hoving, *Tutankhamun: The Untold Story*, p. 209.

48. Quoted in Hoving, *Tutankhamun: The Untold Story*, p. 222.

49. Quoted in Collins and Ogilvie-Herald, *Tutankhamun: The Exodus Conspiracy*, p. 48.

50. Quoted in Mark J. Price, "Curse of the Mummy," *Akron* (OH) *Beacon Journal*, February 5, 2007. www.ohio.com.

51. Quoted in Hoving, *Tutankhamun: The Untold Story*, p. 223.

52. Quoted in Hoving, *Tutankhamun: The Untold Story*, p. 224.

53. Quoted in Vandenberg, *The Curse of the Pharaohs*, p. 24.

54. Quoted in James M. Deem, "Mummy Story 2: The Curse of King Tut's Tomb." www.jamesmdeem.com.

55. Quoted in Vandenberg, *The Curse of the Pharaohs*, p. 25.

56. Quoted in Vandenberg, *The Curse of the Pharaohs*, p. 25.

Chapter 4: Deaths and More Deaths

57. Quoted in Vandenberg, *The Curse of the Pharaohs*, p. 25.

58. Quoted in The Earl of Carnarvon, *No Regrets: Memoirs of the Earl of Carnarvon.* London: Weidenfeld and Nicholson, 1976, p. 126.

59. Quoted in Carnarvon, *No Regrets*, p. 125.

60. Quoted in Collins and Ogilvie-Herald, *Tutankhamun: The Exodus Conspiracy*, p. 85.

61. Quoted in Collins and Ogilvie-Herald, *Tutankhamun: The Exodus Conspiracy*, p. 85.

62. Quoted in Vandenberg, *The Curse of the Pharaohs*, p. 25.

63. Quoted in John Warren, "The Mummy's Curse,"

Tour Egypt. www.touregypt.net.

64. Quoted in Collins and Ogilvie-Herald, *Tutankhamun: The Exodus Conspiracy*, p. 89.

65. Quoted in John Lawton, "The Last Survivor," *Saudi Aramco World*, November/December 1981. www.saudiaramcoworld.com.

66. Quoted in Vandenberg, *The Curse of the Pharaohs*, p. 50.

67. Quoted in Larry Orcutt, "Curses," *Catchpenny Mysteries of Ancient Egypt*. www.catchpenny.org.

68. Quoted in Hoving, *Tutankhamun: The Untold Story* p. 227.

69. Quoted in Orcutt, "Curses."

70. Quoted in *Atlantis Rising*, "King Tut Curse and the Victims." www.atlantisring.com.

71. Quoted in Lee Krystek, "Howard Carter and the 'Curse of the Mummy,'" Virtual Exploration Society. http://unmuseum.org.

72. Quoted in Collins and Ogilvie-Herald, *Tutankhamun: The Exodus Conspiracy*, p. 122.

73. Quoted in Vandenberg, *The Curse of the Pharaohs*, p. 11.

74. Quoted in Cleveland Museum of Art, "Where Were the Pharaohs Buried?" www.clevelandart.org.

75. Quoted in Hoving, *Tutankhamun: The Untold Story*, pp. 229–30.

76. Quoted in Collins and Ogilvie-Herald, *Tutankhamun: The Exodus Conspiracy*, p. 81.

Chapter 5: Magic or . . . What?

77. Quoted in King TutOne, "The Curse of the Mummy." www.kingtutone.com.

78. Quoted in Midnight Fire, "The Curse of Tutankhamun." http://midnight-fire.net.

79. Quoted in Reeves, *The Complete Tutankhamun*, p. 133.

80. Quoted in Reeves, *The Complete Tutankhamun*, p. 135.

81. Salima Ikram and Aidan Dodson, *The Mummy in Ancient Egypt*. London: Thames and Hudson, 1998, p. 137.

82. Quoted in Orcutt, "Curses."

83. Quoted in Collins and Ogilvie-Herald, *Tutankhamun: The Exodus Conspiracy*, p. 92.

84. Quoted in Collins and Ogilvie-Herald, *Tutankhamun: The Exodus Conspiracy*, p. 92.

85. Quoted in Collins and Ogilvie-Herald, *Tutankhamun: The Exodus Conspiracy*, p. 92.

86. Quoted in Brian Handwerk, "Egypt's 'King Tut Tomb Curse' Caused by Tomb Toxins?" *National Geographic News*. http://news.nationalgeographic.com.

87. Quoted in Krystek, "Howard Carter and the 'Curse of the Mummy.'"

88. Quoted in James M. Deem, "Was the Curse of King Tut's Tomb Caused by Anthrax?" Mummy Tombs. http://mummytombs.com.

89. Quoted in Collins and Ogilvie-Herald, *Tutankhamun: The Exodus Conspiracy*, p. 98.

90. Vandenberg, *The Curse of the Pharaohs*, p. 166.

91. Vandenberg, *The Curse of the Pharaohs*, p. 164.

92. Quoted in Vandenberg, *The Curse of the Pharaohs*, p. 177.

93. Quoted in Vandenberg, *The Curse of the Pharaohs*, p. 177.

94. Quoted in Handwerk, "Egypt's 'King Tut Tomb Curse' Caused by Tomb Toxins?"

95. Quoted in Handwerk, "Egypt's 'King Tut Tomb Curse' Caused by Tomb Toxins?"

96. Quoted in Collins and Ogilvie-Herald, *Tutankhamun: The Exodus Conspiracy*, p. 73.

97. Mark R. Nelson, "The Mummy's Curse: Historical Cohort Study," *British Medical Journal*, December 21, 2002. www.bmj.com.

98. Seshat, "Gold and Death—the Secret Curses of the Tomb of Tutankhamun," ThothWeb. www.thothweb.com.

WORKS CONSULTED

Books

Bob Brier, *Ancient Egyptian Magic.* New York: Perennial, 2001.

Bob Brier, *The Murder of Tutankhamen.* New York: G.P. Putnam's Sons, 1998.

Howard Carter and A.C. Mace, *The Discovery of the Tomb of Tutankhamen.* New York: Dover, 1977.

Andrew Collins and Chris Ogilvie-Herald, *Tutankhamun: The Exodus Conspiracy.* London: Virgin, 2002.

Christine Desroches-Noblecourt, *Tutankhamen: Life and Death of a Pharaoh.* London: George Rainbird, 1963.

Elaine Edgar, *A Journey Between Souls.* Lafayette, CO: White-Boucke, 1997.

Christine El Mahdy, *Tutankhamen: The Life and Death of the Boy-King.* New York: St. Martin's, 1999.

Thomas Hoving, *Tutankhamun: The Untold Story.* New York: Simon and Schuster, 1978.

Salima Ikram, *Death and Burial in Ancient Egypt.* Harlow, UK: Longman, 2003.

Salima Ikram and Aidan Dodson, *The Mummy in Ancient Egypt.* London: Thames and Hudson, 1998.

Nicholas Reeves, *The Complete Tutankhamun.* London: Thames and Hudson, 1990.

Philipp Vandenberg, *The Curse of the Pharaohs.* Sevenoaks, UK: Coronet, 1975.

Barry Wynne, *Behind the Mask of Tutankhamen.* London: Souvenir, 1972.

Internet Sources

Atlantis Rising, "King Tut Curse and the Victims." www.atlantisrising.com/the_other_victims_of_king_tut_curse.aspx.

E.A. Wallis Budge, trans., "Papyrus of Ani: Egyptian Book of the Dead" University of Pennsylvania African Studies Center. www.africa.upenn.edu/Books/Papyrus_Ani.html.

Cleveland Museum of Art, "Where Were the Pharaohs Buried?" www.clevelandart.org/kids/egypt/rosefaq.html.

James M. Deem, "Mummy Story 2: The Curse of King Tut's Tomb." www.jamesmdeem.com/museum.mummy2.htm.

James M. Deem, "Was the Curse of King Tut's Tomb Caused by Anthrax?" Mummy Tombs. http://mummytombs.com/news/2001/11.egypt.kingtut.curse.htm.

Brian Handwerk, "Egypt's 'King Tut Tomb Curse' Caused by Tomb Toxins?" *National Geographic News.* http://news.nationalgeographic.com/news/2005/05/0506_050506_mummycurse.html.

Lisa Hopkins, "Jane C. Loudon's *The Mummy!* Mary Shelley Meets George Orwell, and They Go in a Balloon to Egypt." Cardiff School of English, Communication, and Philosophy. www.cf.ac.uk/encap/romtext/articles/cc10_no1.html.

Interesting News Diary, "The Curse of Tutankhamun," August 31, 2006. http://interestingnewsdiary.us/2006/08/curse-of-tutankhamun.html.

King TutOne, "The Curse of the Mummy." www.kingtutone.com/tutankhamun/curse.

Lee Krystek, "Howard Carter and the 'Curse of the Mummy,'" Virtual Exploration Society. http://unmuseum.org/mummy.htm.

John Lawton, "The Last Survivor," *Saudi Aramco World*, November/December 1981. www.saudiaramcoworld.com/issue/198106/the.last.survivor.htm.

Midnight Fire, "The Curse of Tutankhamun." http://midnight-fire.net/shadows/whatrests.html.

Mark R. Nelson, "The Mummy's Curse: Historical Cohort Study," *British Medical Journal*, December 21, 2002. www.bmj.com/cgi/content/full/325/7378/1482.

Larry Orcutt, "Curses," *Catchpenny Mysteries of Ancient Egypt*. www.catchpenny.org/curses.html.

Mark J. Price, "Curse of the Mummy," *Akron* (OH) *Beacon Journal*, February 5, 2007. www.ohio.com/mld/ohio/living/16625468.htm.

Seshat, "Gold and Death—the Secret Curses of the Tomb of Tutankhamun," ThothWeb. www.thothweb.com/article-1636-thread-0-0.html.

John Warren, "The Mummy's Curse," Tour Egypt. www.touregypt.net/featurestories/curse.htm.

Books

Eric H. Cline, *The Ancient Egyptian World*. New York: Oxford University Press, 2005. Examines such aspects of Egyptian life as religion, the arts, medicine, and clothing. Includes a profile of Tutankhamen, among others.

Sylvia Funston, *Mummies*. Toronto: Owl, 2000. Part of the Strange Science series, discusses mummification not only in Egypt but in various other civilizations.

Lorna Greenberg, *Digging into the Past*. New York: Franklin Watts, 2001. Profiles several of the world's most famous archaeologists, including Howard Carter, and their work.

Geraldine Harris, *Ancient Egypt*. New York: Facts On File, 2004. Explores ancient Egypt from a geographical standpoint, supplementing maps with color photographs of various monuments and tombs.

Zahi A. Hawass, *Tutankhamun and the Golden Age of the Pharaohs*. Washington, DC: National Geographic, 2005. Prepared in conjunction with an exhibit of objects from the tomb. Good commentary by one of Egypt's most prominent archaeologists plus a dazzling array of color pictures of objects from the tomb.

Thomas Hoving, *Tutankhamun: The Untold Story*. New York: Simon and Schuster, 1978. A fascinating behind-the-scenes account of the discovery and exploration of the tomb of Tutankhamen.

Salima Ikram and Aidan Dodson, *The Mummy in Ancient Egypt*. London: Thames and Hudson, 1998. Interesting and thorough exploration of mummification, including the religious basis and actual techniques throughout Egyptian history.

Nicholas Reeves, *The Complete Tutankhamun*. London: Thames and Hudson, 1990. One of the most comprehensive accounts not only of the reign of Tutankhamen but also of the contents of the tomb.

Emily Sands, *The Egyptology Handbook*. Cambridge, MA: Candlewick, 2005. Unusual presentation of Egyptology in that it is written from the standpoint of an amateur's journal in 1926.

Richard H. Wilkinson, *The Complete Gods and Goddesses of Ancient Egypt*. New York: Thames and Hudson, 2003. Excellent and well-illustrated examination of religious practices in ancient Egypt, including the integral role religion played in politics.

Web Sites

Ancient Egyptian Culture (www.mnsu.edu/emuseum/prehistory/egypt/archaeology/index.html). Fun site sponsored by Minnesota State University that explores the history of Egyptology and archaeologists, ancient Egyptian technology, archaeological sites, daily life, and "weird theories."

King Tutankhamen (www.crystalinks.com/tut.html). Very good account of Tutankhamen's life, death, and burial on this metaphysical/science site.

Mysteries of Egypt: Tutankhamun (www.civilization.ca/civil/egypt/egtut01e.html). Good survey provided by the Canadian Museum of Civilizations with topics including Tutankhamen's life and times, cause of death, funeral, the tomb and its contents, and the "curse."

Tutankhamun and the Golden Age of the Pharaohs (www.fieldmuseum.org/tut/exhibition.asp). Prepared by the Field Museum to coincide with traveling exhibit of tomb treasures. Fascinating site, particularly the interactive exploration of the tomb.

Valley of the Kings: Tombs of the Pharaohs (http://touregypt.net/kingtomb.htm). This Tour-Egypt site provides descriptions and photographs of various tombs and also multiple links to other information about the individual pharaohs, gods, and so forth.

INDEX

About the Author

William W. Lace is a native of Fort Worth, Texas, where he is executive assistant to the chancellor at Tarrant County College. He holds a bachelor's degree from Texas Christian University, a master's degree from East Texas State University, and a doctorate from the University of North Texas. Prior to joining Tarrant County College, he was director of the News Service at the University of Texas at Arlington and a sportswriter and columnist for the *Fort Worth Star-Telegram*. He has written more than 40 nonfiction books for young readers on subjects ranging from the atomic bomb to the Dallas Cowboys. He and his wife, Laura, a retired school librarian, live in Arlington, Texas, and have two children and three grandchildren.